Russian Tea Time

by

Sharon Bretherick

Copyright © 1998

Turnabout Publishing
202 Tecumseh Drive
Montgomery, AL 33617-4033 USA
334-277-4487

All rights reserved including the right of reproduction in whole or in part in any form.

All scripture is taken from the NIV Study Bible
New International Version
by
Zondervan Bible Publishers
Grand Rapids, Michigan 49506 USA
©1985 by The Zondervan Corporation

ISBN: 1-56325-065-9

Printed in the United States of America

ACKNOWLEDGEMENTS

One person alone does not complete most major projects. In writing this book, I've come to depend on others. I am deeply grateful to Betty Johnsey, my typist; to Judy Harrison, my editor; and to Carolyn Travis, my publisher.

Also, without a vast team of ministry believers, my mission would have been impossible. They have provided both financial and prayer support.

Last but not least, I express my sincere gratitude to my son, Blaine Elliott; my daughter and her husband, Angela and Tim Waldsmith; and my dear, sweet husband, George Bretherick. They have always believed in me.

Thank you all for being God's vessels in this labor of obedience. We pray that this book will be a blessing to many.

INTRODUCTION

Could I have dreamed as an eighth grade student in a small, rural town in Northwest Alabama that I would spend my forty-ninth year in the virtually unknown country of USSR? Is it coincidental that my love for suspenseful reading had propelled me to devour every single book our well-stocked school library possessed on this mysterious country and its infamous KGB? Is it possible in God's sovereignty He was preparing my curious mind to accept His call many years later to serve as a missionary in this intriguing culture? Did our omnipotent Father God plan many years ago for me to record and recount real-life, tea time experiences for enhancing our own relationship with Him?

My husband, George, and I accepted God's definite call in the fall of 1994. Our assignment was to train the Estonian and Russian educators how to teach Christian ethics and morality. George was retiring early, and I was "tying up loose ends" in our successful Christian-based training and development organization. We tearfully bade farewells during the Christmas holidays of 1995 and headed to the Billy Graham Training Center in cold and snowy Sandy Cove, Maryland.

After a few hurried weeks of preparation, we boarded a 747 to carry our team of five into the "wild blue yonder." Our frustration was heightened by the mystique of the snow blizzard, blasting snow horizontally as our plane prepared for landing at the country's national airport in Tallinn, Estonia.

The first step off the plane we were presented with the most beautiful smiles from teammates, each handing us a sweet-smelling, red rose, which we later learned was one of many traditions.

The next several days were filled with acquainting us with more of the Estonian and Russian cultures. The former Soviet Union State, one of the three Baltic States, has a richness of history that boggles one's mind. Of course, the Russian culture is still oozing around every corner and in many homes and neighborhoods of this now free and independent country of Estonia. We were thrilled to learn our new home would be in a Russian community.

As we entered the hallway to our new flat, a stout, gray-haired lady of seventy-something came and greeted us in her native tongue. We responded in our own native tongue, smiling all the while. When I presented her with a new cross lapel pin, she graciously accepted and continued to smile. Her eyes said we were safe. She proceeded to welcome us as she proudly and stoically displayed her Russian Orthodox cross from under three layers of homemade woolens.

Within a few days, our Russian interpreter, MeeMaw (the name our team affectionately gave to her) and I were planning Russian cooking sessions and, of course, traditional afternoon tea times. Tea time is an integral part of Russian culture. Strange as it may seem, many of their frigid, demanding days are steeped in and centered around a robust cup of Russian tea. The strength and flavor of Russian tea represents perfectly the strong, passionate people of a huge, powerful country.

A handful of the hospitable natives as tour guides aided us throughout the year. The next several days of tenure were days of making new acquaintances, finding the "key" contacts to assist us in opening the needed doors, and in saturating us into this vastly different society of tea lovers.

You are probably pondering "then why do we hear so much about Russians and their love of vodka if Russian tea is so hot?" I must sadly report that vodka is just as much of their troubled society as their famous Russian tea. However, in our area of service, we found our environment predominantly saturated with wonderful, rich teas for our enjoyment. Their desire was to respect our preferences.

Russian tea time is when families meet and share the latest happenings and discuss opinions of news reports of this volatile, political climate. Traditionally, neighbors used their tea time as a respite and haven of safety for updates on friends and families involved in the country's numerous skirmishes and revolutions. We were told that during many of their darkest days the women gathered in each other's kitchens (as tiny as they were) and sipped hot tea for hours as they listened to the radios or waited for reports on their own family tragedies.

But just as special are the celebration days of anniversaries, birthdays, and new babies. A Russian birthday is a custom I will never forget. The celebrant prepares food of all kinds for all her friends and family. No matter the weather or workload, one is expected to drop by to spend the day, bearing at least flowers and chocolates. Of course, hot tea is the beverage of choice and is enjoyed by the young and old alike. These are special and joyful days.

Another great joy to the Russian people is reading fine literature. In fact, their literature greats are listed among the grand and noble throughout the world. They are buried in the prestigious cemetery among the great military leaders of years past.

During wartime, books were often confiscated if found by warring parties. Not to be outdone, the clever Russian women would take the saved books to their neighborhood tea time to share with friends, neighbors, and relatives. (Incidentally, a friend or neighbor is treated and respected as family in every way). Actually, they could have called it their own "Tea Time Book Club." Wise mothers believed their children had a chance to survive, even in the worst of times, if they were educated. Much of the education was done in the cozy living rooms while others enjoyed their well-deserved tea time in the kitchen.

The kitchen was so small that most dining was done around a small breakfast table, usually housed in the living room, and in our case, doubled as a table/desk during the many "meeting filled" days and evenings. Just rest assured somewhere on the dining table, if anyone were in the room, were cups of tea flavored with sugar and cream, waiting to be enjoyed. Throughout the centuries the kitchen has remained the favorite place to gather for that longed-for cup of "powerful punch."

Not long after arriving, I was enjoying a hot cup of tea and began to feel dizzy and faint. After a few seconds, I was helped off the stool to a nearby seat. Svettie, our favorite interpreter, asked humorously, "Did you just have some of our tea? It is very powerful, you know?" Yes, I did know, I had just learned it.

As the blizzards continued into what would be early springtime months to us, we had many opportunities to sit, sip, and fellowship with our new friends and acquaintances. These same friends opened many doors for us by invitations to "friends in high places" to join us for, you guessed it, Russian Tea Time. Somehow, God always opened the door for us to tell everyone of His great and awesome love for them. Decisions and commitments to trust God were most often made around a tiny table and a tiny cup of tasteful tea.

Without their gracious hospitality, our mission would have lacked the success we felt was achieved. Without their generous, giving spirit, our year would have certainly been less enjoyable. Russians, one by one, won our hearts. Never did I meet a single Russian I did not like immediately. Their passion and zeal for truth and honesty and their love and pride of country and countrymen will live forever in my heart.

Russian Tea Time is a composite of our experiences, insights, and antidotes God revealed to me as we served a ten-month tenure in Tallinn, Estonia.

Our Russian friends desire their tea to be sipped and enjoyed ever so slowly, tepid to the taste. A fellowshipping occurs between the tea and its lovers. I believe these devotional experiences, if enjoyed in the same delightful manner as Russians relish their tea time, will provide you with a personal and intimate glance into a world once shrouded with mystery.

I pray this book will lead you on a journey to better understand and encounter our grand and glorious God and Savior so that when you know Him more intimately, He will become such an integral part of your everyday life experiences each day will become a flavorful fellowshipping with our fabulous King.

Why don't you pour yourself a cup of your favorite tea, either ice cold or tepidly warm and enjoy with me, *Russian Tea Time*?

1

WE JOURNEY IN J. O. Y.

"Behold I will do a new thing; now it shall spring forth; shall ye not know it? I will even make a way in the wilderness, and rivers in the desert."
Isaiah 43:19

God promised the children of Israel to make a way for them through the desert and to bring them to a new beginning that they might "proclaim my praise."

God has confirmed our commitment to His call by performing glorious acts of kindness through our Christian brothers and sisters. We begin the new year with much excitement and anticipation of our journey with Him.

The "new thing" that shall spring forth may be our intimacy as a "team" couple whose totality of purpose is greater than our individual aspirations. Our team personality may take on an altogether new look -- one that may be difficult to recognize at first glimpse.

Our journey ahead may be a dense wilderness. It may be filled with uncertainty and anxiety. But if we look for His Joy by focusing on Jesus, Others, and You, I am certain rivers in the desert will spring forth like the freshness of dew. There shall be daily refreshment for our thirsty souls. Peace and love will invade each of our cells.

It is our greatest desire that you join us on our journey this year. With Jesus and you traveling along to encourage and confirm us, there truly will be Joy In Our Journey.

Prayer

Oh dear Father, help me not to look for results, or activity, or people to give me worth and joy. May my performance be anchored in my overflow of love for you. May I remember that true Joy comes only from you. Amen.

We do not change by focusing on ourselves or who we are; we change only when we focus on HIM and who He is.

2

TRIUMPHANT JOY

"You will go out with <u>joy</u> and be led forth in peace; the mountains and hills will burst into song before you, and all the trees of the field will clap their hands." Isaiah 55:12

The prestigious leader of Israel is dead. He has been shot down in cold-blooded murder. My heart is saddened as I ponder how God must feel about this barbaric act of outrage.

Our departure date has been finalized. So, it is to be. We will spend an entire year in full-time ministry to the Estonian and Russian peoples.

The combination of the two acts of finality is taking its toll on my usually optimistic demeanor. I can feel myself slipping into a depressed state of mind -- the least of which I need at this hectic time.

Melancholy sets in! How can I leave my family, friends, my future? What must I be thinking? The project of leaving and preparing for such a trip is too great. I cannot handle it. Thoughts of gloom, despair and agony, ooh me. Deep, dark depression, excessive misery...

Suddenly, my heart is drawn to a tiny book lying on our hearth, as it has been for weeks. Absent mindedly, I pick up the book, go to my bedroom, and lock the door behind me. As I begin to read, I know God's spirit is the force behind this "robot like" trance. I read with such vigor and anticipation it startles me. Each page is full of golden nuggets of His wisdom just for me.

And there it is! The "nugget" for which I have been subconsciously searching. It literally jumps off the page as it sears my excited mind. **"Ye shall go out with joy and be led forth with peace."** If it worked for Lettie Cowan, the cofounder of OMS (Oriental Missionary Society as it was called when founded), our sending agency, it will work for me. I shall claim the Word of God just as Mrs. Charles Cowan did in the early 1900's as she set sail to the Baltic States of Latvia, Lithuania, and yes, Estonia. What an awesome God we serve!

Today, my triumphant joy is _____.

Prayer
Oh Father, you blessed Lettie Cowan with a joy and peace that you alone can fully understand. Thank you for empowering me with a similar portion for today. I shall value it as a special treasure, that in order to be enjoyed, must be given away. Father, in this very moment, I claim your peace. Amen.

Something ain't "nothing" until you give it away

3

ANGELS GO BEFORE US

"See, I am sending an angel ahead of you to guard you along the way and to bring you to the place I have prepared." Exodus 23:20

Several times in my life, I have been strangely aware of events, experiences, and episodes that can only be explained by supernatural, unseen forces. I choose to believe the Word of God in regard to this modern day quandary, "Do you believe in angels?"

As I reflect how throughout my lifetime God has fulfilled His promise, I am awed. So, why should I marvel any less in knowing my Heavenly Father, who changes not, has already sent an angel ahead of us to this foreign and strange people?

His promises to guard us along the way provide immeasurable comfort and strength as we face uncertainties and dangers. Just as surely as He has commissioned an angel to prepare the people, circumstances, and events to accomplish His purpose through us, He has commissioned us to be involved in His plan for the Russian/Estonian people.

I have experienced God's protection through His angels when _____

Prayer
Dear Sweet Jesus, thank you for the completeness of this answer; The Lord Himself will be our comfort and adequate supply. Amen.

God's ambassadors

are always

backed by God's

resources

4

FAITH LOOKS INTO TOMORROW

"Now faith is being sure of what we hope for and certain of what we do not see." Hebrews 11:1

I have a new commission. I am being called to something new. At forty-eight, can this continued fervor and passion be from God? Or is it a whim? A passing fury? Mid-life crisis? An emotional need? Actually, God has continued to speak of a "new" thing for me, in me, and through me for several years.

At times it has felt as if God were hiding it from me. I imagine more closely to the truth is His untiring preparation of me. Often times I have wished God would quit giving me so many messages, like the one fourteen years ago during our engagement when He whispered gently as I knelt at our altar for prayer, "Sharon, you and your fiancee, George, will serve me in a full-time training ministry." Neither of us was in the "training" arena at the time, nor did we ever expect to be.

The past has been but a preparation of what lies ahead. His plan has been in embryo stage for many years. Zacharias knew, Mary knew, and I know we have been ordained (probably before I was born), a part in God's worldwide purposes.

We have come to Damascus. Now God will begin to tell us the "things appointed" for us to do.

As I begin a new year, I know I am being called into _____.

Prayer
Father of Heaven and Earth, thank you for planning my life before I was born, for pursuing and wooing me to you even as a child, and for choosing us through which you will demonstrate your awesome power. You alone are worthy to be praised! Amen.

F. A. I. T. H.

<u>F</u>orsaking
<u>A</u>ll
<u>I</u>
<u>T</u>rust
<u>H</u>im

5

DEPARTING ENCOURAGEMENT

"Have I not commanded you? Be strong and courageous. Do not be terrified; do not be discouraged, for the Lord your God will be with you wherever you go." Joshua 1:9

The past few weeks were filled with preparation to leave our home for a year, preparation for Christmas activities, and preparation to bid farewell to friends and family.

Friends searched for meaningful words of comfort. Some succeeded. Family searched for understanding and acceptance, each in his unique and special way. Few shared.

Familiar eyes never pondered more deeply, searching for a connection with my soul. Some found it. The question seemed always to emerge in Christian circles:

> How does one get to the place in his walk with God that enables him to give up everything of familiarity in order to follow Him into an unknown world?

In secular circles, the question was never asked. In fact, the whole subject was ignored as we were dismissed as "having always been crazy."

"The life of fellowship with God cannot be built up in a day. It begins with the habitual reference of all to Him, hour by hour. It then moves on to more and longer periods of communion; and it finds its consummation and bliss in days and nights of intercession and waiting." F. B. Meyer

I may not be able to go to a foreign land, but I can _____.

Prayer

Father God, as others have encouraged me in my step of faith, may I adhere to your divine plan and encourage many as they begin their own unique and special ordained journey with you? Amen.

*Encouraging words,
when received are
like fine silver,
and when given
are more precious
than gold*

6

SLOW ME DOWN, LORD

"'For I know the plans I have for you,' declares the Lord, 'plans to prosper you and not to harm you, plans to give you a hope and a future.'"
Jeremiah 29:11

We never become too old to serve the Lord, but many of us become too busy.

_____ is my greatest hindrance to you, Father.

Prayer

Slow me down, Lord! Ease the pounding of my heart by quieting my mind. Cease my need of hurried pace. Steady my quivering voice as the words roll too quickly. Instill in me a calmness against the confusions of the hour. Change the tension in my nerves and muscles to a soothing sound of song that confines my memory.

Refresh me each day with a child-like passion to fully experience each sidewalk, puddle, fountain of water, and crawling spider. Teach me to look upward often at the long, sturdy branches of the towering oak tree. Remind me how the tree grows stronger because it grows slowly.

Slow me down, again Lord. Instill in me a desire to send my roots into life's fertile soil of enduring passions and causes that I may grow toward the stars of my greater destiny and your greater plan. Amen.

*When it is
Morning - LISTEN*

*When it is
Noonday - THINK*

*When it is
Evening - CONTEMPLATE*

7

THE FRESHNESS OF NEW FALLEN SNOW

*"Cleanse me with hyssop, and I will be clean;
wash me, and I will be whiter than snow."*
Psalm 51:7

I had often wondered what the three weeks of CoMission training could possibly offer from which my husband and I, both seasoned trainers, could possibly benefit. However, the first day of training it became quite obvious that the focus had been firmly established. We were there to be **renewed** and **refreshed**, commonly necessary for a year's commitment of full-time ministry in Eastern Europe.

Midway the morning session, my spirit began to quicken to the pricking of the preciously consistent Holy Spirit. Refreshment! Renewal! Rehabilitation! The first two "R's" seemed much needed, but the third "R" which began the word "Rehabilitation" made a startling suggestion. *I was in need of overhaul!*

As the day continued, the undemanding snowflakes fell ever so softly. My "crud" had overcome me, and I could do nothing better than spend the day in total bed rest. How thoughtful of God to send me such a graphic visual aid. The snow was such a splendid picture of refreshment and renewal. How timely and subtle and beautifully purposeful it was. After careful contemplation, I wondered no longer about the importance and value of the three weeks of training prior to our departure. However, I shall forever be in awe of His love for me and the completeness of His provisions and protection, and His beautiful graphic aids of the freshly fallen snow.

Now, I desire to be cleansed from my _____.

Prayer

Father of all cleansing, as this new year is beginning to unfold, thank you for washing me with your most powerful cleansing agent, the blood of your Son, Jesus Christ! Thank you for the confidence of knowing I am forever whiter and fresher than a new fallen snow. Amen.

You cannot ZIPLOCK your intimacy with God. Each day is a fresh new creation all of its own.

8

JUST DO IT

"So is my word that goes out from my mouth: It will not return to me empty, but will accomplish what I desire and achieve the purpose for which I sent it." Isaiah 55:11

There is an advertisement on television with the key phrase, "Just Do It." In a million years I will not be able to figure why God has called me to serve Him in another country. Nor will I ever comprehend why His will for me is to give up material accumulation, career aspirations, and family connections.

We were preparing to leave for our first year of full-time service by moving our belongings to a storage unit, and I misplaced my key ring. As I fretted over my absentmindedness, it dawned on me that for all practical purposes I had lost nothing. I had no need of the key ring. Our home had been sold; our mailbox key was to be turned in that day; office keys were of no use; cars were to be sold. For the first time in my adult life, I had no need of a key!

My loving and insightful son quickly saved me from despair. "Mother, I've heard that the higher up the ladder you go, the less keys you carry. So, are you so sure you're not close to the top?"

God's promises, scattered throughout both the Old and New Testament, challenge us on what really matters. Even if I can't imagine why He has chosen me, I <u>can</u> be obedient. So, rather than speculate, contemplate, and anticipate, I will "just do it."

Today, in honor of my obedience to you, Father, I will _____.

Prayer

Dear Lord, so many direct questions, so few direct answers. Thank you for trusting me to do what you have chosen me to do. It is such a compliment to be chosen by you. You could have instructed your angels, but instead you have included me in your plan. Amen.

*I tremble
at missing
His guidance!*

9

FAR ABOVE THE BARN LOFT

"You did not choose me, but I chose you and appointed you to go and bear fruit -- fruit that will last. Then the Father will give you whatsoever you ask in my name." John 15:16

At the age of fourteen I knew God had chosen me. I knew not why. As a farmer's daughter my only solitude was in the barn loft among the bails of alfalfa hay. One of my favorite pastimes was standing atop the hay and speaking words of wisdom, hope, and life to the Herefords, horses, hens, and any other critters that happened to be visiting our barnyard.

I pondered often the depths of my young relationship with my Creator. Then it was no less real than now. As I grew in age, I qualified to speak in Christian competitive arenas. The speeches always had an evangelical tone with special appeal to the missionary's passion of reaching the lost in foreign lands. "...but how can they hear without a preacher," was a fragment of scripture that haunted me for years.

Through it all I have felt the touch of my Master's hand. Many times I have questioned, "why"? Often I have tried to shrug it off my shoulder. Sometimes I have purposely tried to become an undeserving creature by creating deliberate acts of disobedience.

But, honestly, my heart has always ached for a more intensely intimate relationship with my Heavenly Father. Such sweet communion I have tasted in difficult seasons of my life, and that made me hungry for more. Such has been my driving passion for a "focused" year of walking ever so closely, hand in hand with Him, far above the barn loft.

I believe God has chosen me to _____.

Prayer

Father, as long as I've walked with you, I've never grown weary of your will and of your ways. Thank you for choosing me to bear your fruit -- fruit that will last forever. Amen.

His will is

the sweetest

thing on earth!

10

UNRESOLVED STUFF

"Search me, O God, and know my heart; test me and know my anxious thoughts. See if there is any offensive way in me and lead me in the way everlasting." Psalm 139:23-24

Prayer

Father God, O Merciful Father, I know you made me perfectly and knew me before I was born. Then influences came and hurts and pains began to shape my mind and behavior. I became less like you and more like me. Then, Father, as you gave birth to my spirit with the blood of your son, Jesus Christ, once again you gave me full permission and confidence to become like you.

Father, I shudder as I earnestly request you to test me. I tremble as I sincerely bequest you to know my anxious thoughts. There is so much of me I still do not understand; so much of you I long to know more intimately.

Fortunately, for me, you are familiar with all my ways. Even before a word is on my tongue, you know it completely. So, Father does this mean my hurtful words can be abolished from my being? Continually remind me to test my actions and see if I am a hindrance to others. Give me the courage to remove them gracefully. Take away my need to dominate and manipulate others. Help me to understand my need, that attempts to be filled with these annoyances, can be fully met in knowing more fully who I am in you and who you are in me.

And lastly, Father, give me courage to approach the throne of grace with confidence so that I may receive mercy and find courage to help me in my time of need. Amen.

One of my most offensive habits to God is _____.

An unbroken vessel is of little use to God!

11

SERVING WITH A PROMISE

"No one will be able to stand against you all the days of your life. As I was with Moses, so I will be with you; I will never leave you nor forsake you."
Joshua 1:5

God made a great promise to Joshua as He commanded this well-prepared warrior to carry on what Moses had begun. Does the same promise stand for us today as we attempt to serve Him with our set of "serving skills"?

Today as my husband and I were commissioned as leaders who are responsible for leading a team of servants into a foreign land, I was reminded of Joshua's model for us.

Will I be as able and ready to lead effectively as Joshua? Will I know inherently what to ask the team members to do as confidently as Joshua seemed? Today as we entered the foreign soil, we began to receive instructions concerning the safety of our teams and the do's and don'ts of correspondence. I was totally surprised there was absolutely no fear residing within me. There seemed to be no fear exhibited by any of the leaders receiving the cautions and instructions.

I have never known a sweeter peace than I've known since answering God's call to become His ambassador to a foreign land. Should I be anxious or scared about our future? I choose to answer the question by posing one of greater substance - <u>Should I believe the inherent infallible Word of God</u>? Should I count on His grace to sustain me each and every day in each minor and major way?

Today, I can serve God by/through

_____.

Prayer

Thank you, my sweet Jesus, for your reminder today. I am not just serving in a foreign land. Rather, I am a servant of our omnipotent Jehovah God, and I am serving with a promise. Amen.

What God commands of us, He also equips us to perform

12

GROWING GRACE FULLY

"I will praise you, O Lord, with all my heart; I will tell of all your wonders. I will be glad and rejoice in you; I will sing praise to your name, O Most High." Psalm 9:1

Spiritual growth always begins with God. He chooses each of us and brings us into a relationship with Him. Our growth is a response to God's Goodness, His Gospel, and His Grace. We desire spiritual growth out of gratitude for what God has done and who He is.

God asks us to join other believers in a regular worship experience, to fellowship with them, to practice prayer, and to live a righteous life style. He brings into our lives people who need us and whom we need. From each other we receive love, nourishment, and comfort. He places us in careers and home environments where we are challenged and confronted to grow, often through pain and conflict.

He challenges us to become more intimate with Him as we become more spiritually disciplined. Our personal development is centered around a motive to "grow more like Him," not to gain fame or self actualization for personal satisfaction. Our spiritual growth embraces all of life. To grow spiritually our lives must come more and more under the lordship of Jesus Christ.

As areas of our lives are claimed by His Lordship, spiritual growth occurs. Our lives become increasingly directed by His spirit. In this refining process, our selfish nature is transformed into caring, our rebellion into obedience, our despair into hope, and our glory into Him. **And wonder of wonders, He does all of this magnificent, graceful work so He can bless us and we can bless others. So spiritual growth begins <u>AND</u> ends with God. We can do nothing to achieve it, earn it, or purchase it. He does it all. He is all. He is fully grace, and he is grace "fully."**

The most recent blessing I received from God is _____.

Prayer

Yes, I'll be ecstatic to praise your name, O Most High. I shall tell of all your wonders and forever praise you, O' Lord, with all my heart. Amen.

Spiritual growth begins in grace, continues through grace, and ends in grace

13

ROMPING WITH THE LIONS

"Praise be to the God and Father of our Lord Jesus Christ, who has blessed us in the heavenly realms with every spiritual blessing in Christ. For he chose us in him before the Creation of the world to be holy and blameless in his sight. In love he predestined us to be adopted as his sons through Jesus Christ, in accordance with his pleasure and will." Ephesians 1:3-5

Have you ever watched a mother lion play roughly and gently simultaneously with her baby cubs? In fun, they entwine each other with gentle, loving movements. But let an intruder abound and the gentle, loving, fondling mother quickly changes into a strong, fierce protector, an absolute authority over her own children.

Can our relationship with our Lord God Jehovah be compared to "romping with the lions"? As we grow into a deeper and more trusting relationship with our Sovereign Lord, our intimacy with Him changes. In our early relationship, most of us see Him as an impersonal God in Heaven, directing all the affairs of men. As we have life's hurdles thrown at us, we must seek beyond ourselves. Finding solitude and help, we begin to think of our Jehovah God as a bit closer in proximity and in spirit. Then a monumental crisis invades our serene and routine day-to-day existence.

Whether it is a job loss, a sudden change in stability brought about by unsettled relationships, or a child dying from cancer, we unashamedly reach for a loving and caring heavenly Father's hand to hold so tightly. It's not long until we realize we are talking to Him often during our days and nights. Such trust develops as we walk and share life together, and it seems rather empty and strange when a day goes by and we fail to get the special sharing time worked into our schedule.

Days and weeks of peaceful existence pass. Hectic days and events subside; we have more freedom to openly express our innermost flaws, doubts, and fears. Actually, it's quite surprising how natural it seems to be so very real and unpretentious.

Years pass and then one day the intimacy is as natural as breathing. Recently, I asked a dear soul mate, my husband, "How do you view my relationship with God?" After a moment of reflecting, he responded, "Yours is one of Romping with the Lion." I smiled and nodded because I knew exactly what he meant.

I describe my intimacy with God as _____.

Prayer

Father and Friend, thank you for creating within us a desire and passion to know you as our Father God and everyday Friend. Thank you for allowing us to be ourselves, sharing, asking, enjoying, and yes, breathing your Life as we breathe ours. Amen.

Intimacy with

our Spiritual

Creator should

be as natural

as laughing

and breathing

14

TO FEEL GOD'S PLEASURE

"How great is the love the Father has lavished on us, that we should be called the children of God!"
I John 3:1a

Have you ever stopped to think about your attributes that give God great pleasure? Most of us are so busy criticizing what we do and say that displeases our Heavenly Father we forget the importance of seeking "to feel His Pleasure." Perhaps it is just as relevant to our spiritual growth for us to feel His Pleasure as it is for Him to be pleased.

As I have contemplated this fresh new phrase, I find it a difficult concept to ponder. More basically, I've come to realize that I feel His pleasure when I touch another of His lovely and unique creatures, especially one who only receives an occasional touch, like an elderly person begging for pennies. I feel this pleasure when I stop and watch an innocent, small child pondering his new world.

Recently, I've felt God's pleasure through sensing in my memory book all those unique aromas of my childhood home: my mother's special cinnamon and chocolate sugar roll, my daddy's "pine kindling" fire prepared for us on a cold and early morning, and those large, delicious Florida oranges and grapefruits ordered by the school's agricultural department for enjoyment during the blessed Christmas season. I'm beginning to feel His pleasure when I stop, become very quiet and still, simply to be in His presence.

I sense His greatest pleasure when after prayer, study, and contemplation, I attempt to express myself to Him. His greatest pleasure seems to be mine to enjoy of the greatest immensity when I pen my conversations with Him. When do you sense His greatest pleasure?

I feel His greatest pleasure when I _____.

―――――∽∞∽―――――

Prayer
So the question is this Father. Does it cause you great pleasure for us to want to sense or feel your pleasure? If it does Father, would you teach me to open my heart and mind to finding more and more pleasurable ways for me to sense your pleasure? Amen.

The aromas of home are life's most lasting memories

15

LET THE SNOW FALL!

"I have learned in whatsoever state I am in, therewith to be content." **Philippians 4:11**

Upon arriving at our temporary home, a conference and retreat center on the Eastern seaboard of Chesapeake Bay, we learned several startling facts that would definitely present a challenge.

Not only was there no TV (which meant no CNN news to put me to sleep or wake me as usual), but neither was there radio or newspapers available. Then to add insult to injury, there was no coffee maker with several coffee or tea flavors available.

As I was absorbing all this disturbing information concerning our accommodations, it began to snow heavily. Since we had arrived at the lodge by shuttle from the airport after dark, the out of doors remained somewhat a mystery while the twenty-seven inches of snow lingered.

What was God trying to say to me? Why so aggressive approach to communicate His message? Wasn't the change of culture that was facing us not enough of a challenge?

As the most beautiful snowfall I ever hoped to experience continued, I began to reflect and contemplate just what lay before us in our year of ministry with the Estonian people.

Ten days passed. The only bombardment of sounds were the classical music tapes we played on our tape recorder. My thoughts were conversations with my Heavenly Father.

After long hours of training and spiritual preparation for working with the spiritually starved Estonians, I was rejuvenated as I recorded significant thoughts and insights in my spiritual journal. *The USA Today* seemed to be somewhat less relevant to our newly chosen world.

Sunday afternoon my hubby and I romped in the snow as if we were children. We even threw snowballs! In a quiet time of reflection, these questions formed: "Dear Sharon, what was it you kept telling me was the desire of your heart? Can't you see why I'm giving you this special preparation time with an environment so uncluttered as the one to which you had grown accustomed? You asked for a year of greater intimacy with me as you serve me one year, totally focused on me. Didn't you? You first must learn to be content with just me."

Today, I must begin to be content with _____.

Prayer

Oh my, Sweet Jesus. You have already begun to give me what I asked for. How like you to give us our desires when we delight ourselves in you. Thank you for giving me such contentedness. Such joy and peace. What a year I am about to experience in the frigid Northern Baltic State of Estonia. Let the snow fall! Amen.

God +

nothing -

nothing =

Everything

16

MY NEW OUTFIT

"Put on the full armor of God so that you can take your stand against the devil's schemes."
Ephesians 6:11.

What is your favorite piece of clothing or jewelry? Maybe it's a hat or a broach left for you by your beloved grandmother. Maybe it's a pair of worn out sweats or a pair of well-worn jeans.

In my early twenties my clothes became my god. They were all I thought about. Which piece of jewelry and shoes would go with which skirt or suit? Never did one see me wear the exact same outfit twice. I made sure of it!

About five years ago, I heard God's voice commanding me to begin to rid myself of so much "stuff," so many clothes. Although I did not understand at first, the message was very clear. As I began to sort through my over-crowded closets, I learned a lot about myself.

There were just a few colors that I preferred - I would allow myself to wear only those colors that flattered me. I observed that there were very few styles, mostly of a "classic" nature, that would project the image I wanted. There was definitely a pattern to the lengths of skirts and dresses. Overall, there was a distinct look to what I had chosen as "my" outfits.

This image, I had surmised, would be the one to get me where I wanted to go in life and help to keep me there.

Since arriving in the foreign and distinctly different culture, my favorite outfits have changed. My favorite ones are of different color, texture, and shape than I have chosen in the past. My outfit for the extreme cold has become special to me as it protects me daily from the bitter chills and winds of the Baltic Sea. The coat is specifically designed to protect from wind, rain, and cold. But just as important, but less cumbersome, are the wool mittens and wide, long wool scarf, the wool hat, and the wool leggings.

With one piece of our outfit missing, we cannot survive, once outside. We only forget that piece once! Even though it demands much effort and time each morning to properly equip ourselves for the day's temperature, the decision to survive and stand firm has already been made. It must be done!

My favorite "inner outfit" has much of the same characteristics. The belt of truth, breastplate of righteousness, feet fitted with readiness, the shield of faith and the helmet of salvation. Each piece of this outfit is critical and performs a certain function in our daily and spiritual life. The entire outfit gives full and adequate protection. With one piece missing, our outfit cannot protect us fully from the spiritual warfare we are bound to encounter. We dress in a proactive mode for our inner protection the same as we do for our outer protection. When the time comes, we will be prepared. Having dressed properly, we can focus on "being," not on what we need to wear for protection.

Clothing here is much different from the states. My current outer wardrobe is quite slim: two jackets, two skirts, one pair of jeans, one pair of slacks, a couple of blouses and sweaters. It's been quite a while since I've had a new piece of jewelry or a new blouse. My "inner outfit" has become much more important to me lately. <u>In fact, it has become my very favorite outfit!</u>

The piece of my spiritual outfit that is missing is _____.

Prayer

Father, today, before I do one more thing, I realize that this piece of my spiritual outfit is missing. Will you please replace and restore it? Then I shall be complete...lacking nothing! Amen.

Clothes <u>can</u> make the man if God designed the outfit

17

MEEMAW, MAXX, AND ME

"Always giving thanks to God the Father for everything, in the name of our Lord Jesus Christ."
Ephesians 5:20

"God, are you sure you know what you are doing? From the first day of arriving in Tallinn, Estonia, and settling into our eleventh-floor flat, I have constantly asked you Why? Why this flat Lord?"

One of my most often quoted scriptures comes to mind. It is something about "if we delight ourselves in Him, He will give us the desires of our heart." Should I be so bold as to tell God this raggedy, dirty old flat is not exactly pleasing to my heart? If we have to be away for a whole year, couldn't we at least be in one where wallpaper and tile match? Matters worsened when we visited our teammates' flats. They are so comfortable, lovely, and even located in a residential community.

Because of our feeling less than safe, a friendship began the first time my neighbor, whose flat is behind the same locked door as ours, appeared in the hallway. An elderly Russian widow I'll affectionately call MeeMaw hastily reached for her Russian Orthodox cross when I presented her with a small lapel cross. There was a stern and worn woman outside, but a kind and loving heart, I surmised.

I began to pray God would use our neighbor to open doors for His ministry here in this community of Russian people still living in Estonia. I continued to ask God to give me wisdom in ways to build a solid relationship. And, as usual...He was faithful to hear and answer us according to His will.

Much to my delight, food was the answer! As the friendship quickly grew, a spirit of bonding and respect concreted. I decided to ask her (through our interpreter) to teach me to prepare her favorite Russian traditional recipes. She quickly and eagerly agreed.

The first afternoon she taught me the skill of making the famous Russian soup, borscht. I felt an unexplainable kindred as she departed with the task successfully completed. The second dish was a Russian bliny - a pancake-like delicacy served at formal occasions. Those were delivered and served hot without warning. There were no complaints from our kitchen!

The third experience was accompanied by Maxx, her "loveliest" of grandsons. Maxx is a fifteen-year-old student of a "Classical University" for advanced students. He is very intelligent, well mannered, and very proud of his family traditions. The day's project was the popular Russian "pelmeni" - a dumpling dish that takes hours to prepare.

As the dish was being prepared, Maxx seemed to enjoy the task of interpreting and often interjecting his own well-prepared questions. "Why are you here in my country?" "How long?" "Why would you want to help my people?" and on and on.

About four hours later, we served the pelmeni to George, MeeMaw, Maxx and me with candlelight and classical music. We laughed, ate, laughed, and ate some more, until no more pelmeni could be eaten!

The wonderful evening came to a close, and we exchanged our pleasantries. George and Maxx had planned for ongoing exchange of computer training and bird watching. MeeMaw and I had bonded to a solid level of trust. This time her hug was accompanied by a great big kiss.

As I closed the door after watching them safely enter their own, I heard myself say to George, "Now I know why God wanted us in this flat! He definitely has plans for MeeMaw, Maxx and Me!"

Suddenly, the dirty, ragged old flat seemed to take on a brighter, livelier look, a look quite pleasing to me.

Today I thank you Lord for my neighbor, _____ .

Prayer

Oh precious all-knowing Father. Thank you for this raggedy old flat. Thank you for our wonderful caring neighbor. Thank you for what you are doing this year. We praise you in the name of our Lord Jesus Christ as we learn to thank you for everything! Amen.

Praise

the

Lord,

anyhow!!!

18

MARY, SWALLOW THOSE "T'S"

"Jesus answered, 'I am the way and the truth and the life. No one comes to the Father except through me.'" John 14:6

Have you ever tried to master a foreign language? The Estonian language is recognized as one of the most complex in the world. Nevertheless, in part to show our great respect for the culture and people of Estonia, we agreed to tackle an intense 110 hours of language. Even though the language is derived from our alphabet, each vowel is sounded differently. In addition, each syllable is heard; only consonants are "swallowed." Often, though, consonants such as Ts and Ls are not strongly pronounced.

Each of our team seemed to have his own demon to overcome in learning this difficult, fifteen-case language. For Denise it was the rolling of the Rs, for me it was not swallowing the consonants, but for Mary a very difficult one of not swallowing her Ts plagued her throughout the whole course.

As I awakened each morning, I could hear our teacher correcting Mary in her usual forthright manner, "Mary, Mary, those Ts, those Ts, don't swallow your Ts." Mary would graciously smile, acknowledge, and correct her current usage of the letter T.

With the great complexities of the rigorous first few weeks, I began to dwell on what all those Ts could represent. Why was not swallowing those Ts so important? Certainly we have had to swallow many. **Tiredness** has been a great thing to overcome with the demands of training plus settling into a new home, new everything. **Temptations** of not focusing <u>on who we are and whose we are</u> have been difficult to withstand. **Tongue** usage of complaining and whining has been swallowed to please our Lord. **Training** has been long and arduous. Swallowing our own decisions and needs to focus during this critical time of conditioning and preparation has been vital. **Tantrums** have emerged and have been swallowed as we were extremely stressed. **Team relationships** have been built and nourished. Self and self needs have become no longer acceptable in our team environment. **Tension** has abounded. Each of us has been stressed for our own reasons. We have begun to feel each irritation from the others, none in ourselves. **Things** we have never had to do without-like ZIPLOCK bags, no-stick cooking spray, and good emery boards, we have longed for. **Thanksgiving** has been swallowed as we have taken residence on Pitiful Me Avenue. Lastly, the **Truth** is that our Heavenly Father has promised that <u>He</u> is the Way, Truth and Life.

Today, I will make myself aware of _____, the T most important for me to remember today.

Prayer

*Righteous and merciful Father, forgive me as I deal with those **Ts** to stay focused on you. Help me to rely on your strength in this time of personal weakness. Give me enough strength for **Today**. May I never swallow the **T** in Today. It is all I have. It is your cross, your gift to us. Only through focusing on the cross can we truly have your strength within us to endure. Amen.*

The greatest

T

there is to

swallow is the

one in cross.

19

GOD IS HOME - ALL HIS LIGHTS ARE ON!

"And God said, 'Let there be lights in the expanse of the sky to separate the day from the night, and let them serve as signs to mark seasons and days and years, and let there be lights in the expanse of the sky to give light on earth.' And it was so."
Genesis 1:4-5

While riding in the car one clear summer night, our daughter, Angela, just four, gazing at the star-spangled sky, shouted, "God's home; all His lights are on."

In order to have a quiet time with God before we are due at language training, we must arise before five o'clock. As I look out across the horizon from my eleventh-floor flat, there is a myriad of lights shining brightly across the sky. Some of these beautiful shimmering bulbs are man made with many flaws, but still perform a much needed function. Others are inside homes and serve to warm and enlighten one's haven of security. Then there are those lights that majestically hang in the heavens just doing their usual thing - "separating the day from night" - and, in general, acting like connectors keeping God's universe together.

Once I have my habitual, aromatic cup of Maxwell House and I begin to focus my thoughts on what I do see, a comforting deluge of peace and serenity abound as I automatically and unconsciously check to see if all God's lights are on. What a joy to know no matter what our past has been, how many times we missed opportunities to share our joy and love for the Lord we can in full assurance come to "The Light Designer." And best of all, we can know with perfect certainty that He's home; all His lights are on all the time!

Father, this morning I want to especially thank you for your light of _____.

Prayer
Dear sweet Father, thank you for your dependability of always being available. You are ten million times better than CNN news that I have missed so much and usually spent my A.M. time enjoying. Thank you for hanging those lights out so we can be assured you are definitely always home. Amen.

His light shining

in me can be

a connector that

helps hold

someone's world

together

20

PINE THICKET PHENOMENON

"The Lord is my rock, my fortress and my deliverer; my God is my rock, in whom I take refuge." Psalm 18:2a.

As a child my father's pine thicket always fascinated me. Being the only girl at home with three brothers, the farm's beautiful pine thicket often served as my haven of escape. Those many pines standing so perfectly still and doing absolutely nothing but "being" were grand listeners. They listened as I shared the sorrows and the disappointments of my confused, impressionable heart.

"My" pine thicket was unique because of its rows of ridges, designed to keep the ground from washing away beneath the trees. Those ridges were great couches, and the mounds of pine straw were great cushions. I talked to God, questioned Him with many profound theological issues and tried to make sense out of my existence and His. Those planned rows of pines, planted in a design to serve as a straight line from any direction, served often as an amusement and a wonderment for my young, analytical mind. Why was each pine so similar but so different? How does a pine tree feel being so destined to its lifestyle? What makes one tree a tiny bit different but so similar to all the others?

Here in Estonia, behind our daily bus stop, is a thicket of beautiful, growing, young pine trees. I have been drawn to lose myself in them many times as I have waited for Bus # 10.

Yesterday I was again drawn into their captivity. As always a comfort and peace soothed me as I was mentally and spiritually led away to enjoy their splendor of design, color, and anonymity. Each pine is so very beautiful. Each is independent on any other pine, but its strength is illuminated and heightened with the remaining pines firmly planted in either direction.

Being so captivated, I began to carefully inspect each pine. I found each to possess a unique design and personality all its own. Each has its strength; each has its flaws. Each is independently strong but even stronger from being part of the thicket. A body of trees with a common purpose and strength add to the individual beauty.

The aromas of the strategically planted pine thicket flooded my being with total awe and amazement of our Creator. My Creator is even more dependable and timely than the arrival of ole Bus # 10 that carefully pulls to a deliberate stop.

Today my favorite place of peace and solitude is _____.

Prayer

Thank you, Heavenly Father. Even when I am thousands of miles from home, you surround me with places of beautiful reminders of childhood peace, security and warmth. You, alone, are my protection and strength. Amen.

Jesus is our rock, our sure foundation against everyday storms

21

BAKING FOR SERVICE

Suppose one of you wants to bake a cake. Will you not find a recipe, sit down to study it and make a list of the ingredients to make sure you get all that is needed from the grocery store.
Luke 14:28
Paraphrase by George Bretherick.

Grocery shopping is not one of my favorite tasks. Okay, I admit it, neither is the daily chore of cooking. But now baking is another story, especially if time allows for experimenting with a new recipe, all the ingredients, neatly packed away in cabinet space, are awaiting the experiment **and** the recipe is clear and simple to interpret! Not too much to ask, is it?

After getting settled the first few weeks in this strange, new world of ours, I couldn't wait any longer to see if any creativity was left in this soul of mine. So off to the grocery store I went, once I had decided on a traditional cake recipe my Russian neighbor had given me. She had translated it into English just for me. Sounds easy? Yeah, until I got to the store only to find <u>none</u> of the items in the grocery market aisles were in English. Hours were spent deciding which packages contained cinnamon, nutmeg, baking powder, and all the other specific ingredients needed to make this mouthwatering apple cake - one of my husband's favorites.

As I began to experiment with the spices and sifted what appeared to be a type of flour, an analogy much more important than my apple cake began to transform me and continues to do so till this day. **GOD IS BAKING A CAKE WITH EACH OF OUR LIVES!** He chooses some ingredients, of which we would never think, to create His masterpiece. Some are sweeteners; others are spices, and other ingredients are used simply for balance and stability, not unlike salt and baking powder in my apple cake.

At times when He speaks to us through life's experiences, we need an interpreter, a wise Christian friend, to translate into a word picture what makes sense to us. The blending of the bad ingredients with the good ones is divinely intended.

Of course, with any cake that is baked, there is some point when that blended creation must enter the extreme heat of the oven. Never in all our wishing will it come out a beautifully luscious blend of exquisite aroma and taste without the precisely selected temperature for a specifically selected amount of time.

With the perfect recipe, the exactness of blending, the carefully chosen ingredients, the correct amount of each ingredient, the selected time and temperature for baking, and <u>Honey, watch out!</u> <u>You will come out of that oven smoking!</u> A true masterpiece indeed! Just in time for <u>Serving</u>!

The ingredient God is adding to my "cake" in my present circumstances is _____.

Prayer
*Father God, thank you for each ingredient you have very carefully chosen for my baking. I trust you completely to create your Masterpiece with my life. My life is yours, and my desire is to end this race "**smoking!!!**"* Amen.

God is using ingredients from all languages and cultures to form His final product

22

A SWEET, SWEET SPIRIT

"In the same way, let your light shine before men, that they may see your good deeds and praise your Father in heaven." Matthew 5:16

A few of my best friends have a sweet and kind nature. Others are sweet and kind on occasion. Depending on whether it's a good "hair day" or "bad hormone day," almost no one seems to possess a spirit in which struggling to be sweet is part of daily life -- except me!

Of course, I have conjured up some very good and reasonable explanations for my less than "sweet spirit," based upon childhood experiences, parent rejections, and struggles as a child. Since I don't have time to announce these justifications to all the souls along my "less-than-sweet, day-to-day experiences," I must ask God to p-l-e-a-s-e change me!

I have been asked to be a key note speaker for a Christian Women's Conference upon my return to the states. Ironically, the theme of the conference is "A Sweet, Sweet Spirit." To be qualified to speak on the topic, one should be able to demonstrate a sweet spirit if not always, at least periodically, don't you think?

Pondering this thought has often led me to pray for God to change me from my bone marrow to my epidermis. What better place to perfect "this" work in this charred and broken vessel than a foreign culture? Daily God reminds me of the importance of being His chosen vessel for these downtrodden people. **To these people, His people may stand in the place of God!** We may be the only Bible they read, all of Jesus they will see. What a chance to demonstrate a sweet, sweet spirit.

It is vital that we represent the Lord accurately by giving those around us a glimpse of who Jesus is. Today, I commit my life anew to Christ likeness and trust Him to develop in me a sweeter and sweeter spirit as others see Him in me.

If I could master _____, my spirit would be sweeter.

Prayer

Oh Lord, do not rebuke me in your anger, nor chasten me in your Hot displeasure. Have mercy on me, O' Lord, for I am weak; O Lord, heal me for my bones are troubled, my soul is greatly troubled. But you, O Lord...how long? Psalms 61:3. Amen.

A sweet, sweet

Spirit creates

an aroma

which will make

a God-like

environment

23

INTRODUCTION RUSSIAN STYLE

"Let your conversation be always full of grace, seasoned with salt, so that you may know how to answer everyone." Colossians 4:6.

Last Friday I was asked to represent our team with a Russian interpreter at a school (which shall remain nameless) for celebration of its name change. I had no idea what to expect and was not sure why we were going, but this is a school in which one of our team members, who is on R & R, has been training.

We were greeted at the front door, as were all the dignitaries, and escorted to the filled auditorium's front seats. Immediately, my interpreter turned to me and frantically exclaimed, "They want you to make a speech. Can you do that?" I assured her "we" could do that, but I needed to know what they expected.

As the other dignitaries, including the Mayor and Minister of Education, made their speeches and presented their flowers and expensive gifts to the school's Director, the interpreter translated a summary statement. She spent the rest of our translation time filling me in on the political climate, our history with the school, etc.

They even had arranged for a student to translate all the special announcements for me, and for the school ensemble to sing an English ballad, "My Bonnie Lies Over The Ocean." I was moved to tears by their efforts. I have never depended on God and His word any more than during those endless three to five minutes. The words "through His strength" and "when I am weak He is made strong," took on a new and greater meaning.

I told them I was part of a team from the U.S., and I brought them greetings from that team. Applause was immediate! I said I had come to learn from them much about their passion, pride and love of culture, tradition, history and love of country. We had brought some resource materials for teaching they might enjoy. And I shared with them that my dream of coming to their country began when I was fourteen, and that it had motivated me to read all my school's library books on their country and culture. Another applause!

I shared how through God's grace and a large team of people who cared as much as I that today, with snow-filled woods and meadows, my dream was coming true. I said I looked forward to an exciting year of sharing and learning together much about love, pride and love of God and country. They clapped again. I was touched. Moreover, I knew without a doubt I was home - my new home to which God had called me.

The reason so much fanfare about the name change is that the Estonian government has agreed to allow a certain number of Russian Schools to remain purely Russian forever! They will never be forced to change to the Estonian culture and tradition. Therefore, the celebration was done with total Russian tradition and formality in black and white attire with a formal reception following! What a treat it was for my very first introduction into this complex and amazing world of Eastern Europe.

Today, I feel the most like my call of God is
_____ .

―――――∽∞∾―――――

Prayer
Father of all peoples, thank you for calling me to such a beautiful land and giving me a passion for its people. Thank you for their acceptance of me. Thank you for the snowy woods and meadows. And lastly, Father God, thank you for giving me your words. You alone are my reason to give hope! Amen.

Be Sure you

know who

you are before

you try to

tell others!

24

CREATED TO BE LOVERS

"Dear friends, let us love one another, for love comes from God. Everyone who loves has been born of God and knows God. Whoever does not love does not know God, because God is love. This is how God showed his love among us: He sent His one and only Son into the world that we might live through him. This is love: not that we loved God, but that he loved us and sent his Son as an atoning sacrifice for our sins. Dear friends, since God so loved us, we also ought to love one another." I John 4:7 - 11

God created us to be lovers! Think about it! Why else would our whole of existence center around relationships? In His divine omnipotence and omniscience, God created us to be lovers of God, lovers of self, and lovers of others.

Why is the whole of creation centered around this emotion called love? I have often pondered this question but no longer, for this one simple explanation.

What I **haven't** quite figured out is why then, did He reverse the order and design us biologically to begin life totally and completely as a lover of self. If you are like most of us and cannot remember when you were first introduced to this world, think about young children you know, perhaps your own. Are they not totally absorbed in what they want and need?

After attending a newborn's needs for a few hours, no one could dispute my claim that we enter this world with only one clue about this subject of love. My needs are all that matter. In fact, I dare say not one other concern enters the minds of us as children until we've been here for quite a while.

Somewhere along the way a still small voice begins to direct and guide us into a search for love much beyond our own needs. In fact, if we are wise and listen carefully, we will be guided into much depth and understanding about loving relationships. Our family, colleagues and mankind as a whole become important, loving relationships. Those mature relationships route us to a deeper search and meaning to life, which leads us to become greater lovers of God.

You may disagree with the order of which comes first, love of people or love of God. For me, it was a simultaneous emerging. For you it may be quite different. I have come to recognize my love of self, others, and God are interdependent in depth, maturity, and satisfaction.

Nevertheless, as God's spirit in us matures, we become more and more attuned to the needs of others, and less and less concerned about needs of our own. Ideally, God intends for us to become so balanced in the "love" base that there is a perfect balance. Oh, selfish one, don't get too excited. It is not an equal balance for God, self, and others. God created us to be lovers perfectly balanced by His calculations. God first, others second, and ourselves last.

Have I convinced you that God created us to be lovers? If not, continue contemplating this awesome subject as you read I John 1, 2, and 3. If we are created in His image and GOD IS LOVE, then how can our creation be for anything else than to be lovers?

Today, I believe my love balance is _____.

Prayer
Master Lover, Creator of all Lovers, thank you for loving me, creating me, and creating me to love you, others, and myself in your perfectly balanced plan. Amen.

Christian love

is basically

a response

to God's love!

25

"STUFFLINKS" OR "CUFFLINKS"

"Who being in very nature of God, did not consider equality with God something to be grasped, but made himself nothing, taking the very nature of a servant being made in human likeness." Philippians 2:6-7

Entering into a new culture can produce fright and uncertainty as well as shock. But entering a new world of people and values can be less scary if one comes packed with a few comforts from home. We have become accustomed to these comforts and call them necessities for a good reason: We <u>think</u> they are!

As we transitioned from our comforts of home into a "step back in time," I carefully calculated what it would take to "give my year to God," simultaneously keeping enough of my world to feel connected. As the suitcases of "stufflinks" were unpacked and placed in appropriate shelves and drawers, each "stufflink" needed to be checked for possible damage from traveling.

The computer would be my number one "stufflink" because, via e-mail, "God's manna to the 90's," this mamma, friend, and loyal family member would stay very connected to home. Those many books were purposely placed in my carefully chosen "reading and quiet spot" (which took me two weeks to find). Of course, number one "stufflink," our computer would serve us well in this costly endeavor. A high-priced camcorder had been purchased to provide high quality connectedness to our ministry team.

All of my "connections" did not come from home. Some were already here, I had reckoned, like the postal and phone system. And, of course, with a good refrigerator I could enjoy a few quality food items that could be sent via "care packages" from all our caring and loyal friends and family.

Within the first three weeks, those precious "stufflinks" became tools in which God had chosen to continue His work for this one-year journey. Our water quit continuously; the <u>phone</u> service was disconnected due to unpaid bills of $700 U.S. dollars charged by a prior renter. The expensive <u>camcorder</u> was dropped and broken by my husband, the computer and printer had untraceable "bugs," the refrigerator decided to rest hours during the day, ruining most of our "good" food items, and finally, e-mail seemed to be an impossibility as well as did receiving mail.

As I quietly sat during my "quiet time" and searched for meaning through the various scriptures, the veil began to dissipate. How <u>can</u> God use me as long as I am hanging on to those precious "stufflinks" of mine? Without humbling myself and developing the same servant's attitude as lowly and meekly as Jesus did, how can I enter into His presence? How can I become like Him?

It dawned on me. Entering into His presence must be with a humble heart with no strings, no stufflinks -- but total dependence on Him and His awesome power to do His work in and through me.

Jesus, empower me to release my need for _____
_____.

Prayer
Father of all stuff, please release my desire for stuff, release my needs to be linked to the comforts of home, and create a heart with no strings attached. Amen.

STUFF<u>LINKS</u>

only link you to

STUFF

-- not God!

26

"STIFFNECKED," "STRESSED," OR "STRAINED?"

"Therefore each of you must put off falsehood and speak truthfully to his neighbor, for we are all members of one body." Ephesians 4:25

As we began to function as a group of individuals placed together to accomplish the common goal of ministry, the tremendous task that lay ahead became quite clear.

The makeup of the individuals' personalities made it obvious from the onset that our work was cut out for us. Within hours we saw and heard numerous remarks and quips that concerned us. The concern was based on what the remarks represented -- rebellion to structure, to rigidity, to authority! Oh, I had prayed we had "misread" the signs, but deep within my heart I was certain we were headed for a tumultuous year.

The second week of training was reaching its conclusion; people were tired and already showing obvious signs of noncommitment, nonparticipation, and just plain determination not to like anything leadership stood for or was attempting to provide in training. As the team discussed the nonissues, the "real" issues became evident. There was definitely an agreed-upon issue of stiffnecked attitudes, sheer rebellion to authority and all it represented.

Later, pondering all the remarks carefully, I stared quietly at the fresh falling snow outside the trolley window. I wondered if the tinge of despair and hurt I was feeling was akin to my Father God's as He tries so desperately to break through to a stiffnecked world of stubborn mankind. Mankind thinks our way is right, we know best, and we'll prove it by doing things our way! Later as I quietly prayed for wisdom in how to meet the needs of the team's individuals, a kaleidoscope of our first month together began to spiral quietly through my mind. Conclusion! - The team members are "stiffnecked" or "strained" from the culture shock and stress of the decision and commitment they have made.

This week I feel stress about _____.

Prayer

Dear Lord, What have we got ourselves into? Why? Lord, Why? Do we want so to do it our way, not Yours? Help me Lord! Amen.

We don't need information, we need transformation.

Joyce Meyer

27

THE MASTER GOLD MAKER

"He will sit as a refiner and purifier of silver, He will purify the Levites and refine them like gold and silver." Malachi 3:3

God is the master gold maker, the refiner, the purifier. If we yield to His molding, He will continue to perfect us. How long is the process? For me, it will take a long time, more years than has already been, I'm sure. The master gold maker has all the time in the world to wait and perfect one into the ideal image.

Some lessons take longer than others. A few lessons can be learned instantly, but others, usually the major ones, may take the Master Gold Maker's heating the furnace hotter and hotter until that one ugly corner has been fired away forever.

Oh, what love! Even on our most mundane days, our jeweler is waiting in a most patient love to add some new touch to our strength and beauty. Sometimes we lull ourselves into thinking all the details of our day are mere happenings, coincidences, incidents and mishaps, caused by our own efforts. But after a while, a wise one recognizes He is molding and making a perfect image.

If the one receiving the refining could understand life as the Master Gold Maker does, he would look for His finishing in each of life's details and in every circumstance.

If one could see the gracious Maker's intent, each unfriendly blow of the chisel would be met with a welcomed shield and armor prepared for the firing of that experience, only to proclaim at the onset, "nothing can move me."

Prayer

Dear Master Chisler of my life, thank you for your continual patience with even the minute details that need refining. To the masses, my stone may resemble a high quality even now; but to those who receive me in my lowest times, the remaining rough edges need to be severed. I await with anticipation the continuation of a lifelong process. Each flaw that hinders your perfect image will be fired and chiseled until <u>you</u> and you <u>alone</u> are pleased. Amen.

Formulas will never replace the Freshness of God's daily love.

28

WHERE ARE THE NATASHAS?

"The least of you will become a thousand, the smallest a mighty nation. I am the Lord; in its time I will do this swiftly." **Isaiah 60:22**

Culture Shock is dissipating. As language training is nearing an end, a yearning deep in my heart begins to emerge. The yearning is my spirit's groaning for this stiffnecked people and downbeat culture.

Surely, God has been at work mightily for the past few months and years in Eastern Europe. We keep hearing the stories that inspire us to "keep the faith" and continue our obedience. One of the OMS leaders reports this conversation with a Russian teacher at a convocation: "Three years ago I attended a convocation here, and I heard the name JESUS. I longed to know more about this name of which I knew nothing. Today I have come back to hear more about the name JESUS. I have been waiting for you. Thank you for coming."

One interpreter reported this: "If communism ever returns, it is for certain we will be killed for being so outspoken. We know they have a list of our names, but it is no worry. We have found so much more than human freedom. We know we will see you again, someday."

A driver responded the following to a Christian who was commenting on the country's progress since his last visit: "Thanksgiving and Christmas holidays you have just had. Someday we will have them too, and they will be nice. You see progress on the outside; we need to feel in here (pointing to his heart) something new. It still not feels good."

Among the masses, on the crowded trolleys, trams, and busses, there are many faces with lines that make them seem so much older than their years. There are bent postures and joints that have taken on new looks from wear and tear of seasons of bitter weather and bitter hearts.

Occasionally, though, there is a face with all its wear, still beaming brightly. A flicker of hope illuminates the space around it. My yearning is pricked. Instantly, I sense a kindred spirit and begin to wonder if this is the heart that God has heard. Are these the knees that have dented hard, uncovered wooden floors at home and in secret meeting places for many seasons? Was it Olga, or Zoya, or Leena, or Madli, or Natasha (None of the names are connected to the stories selected), that stole the heart of God for this people?

Prayer

Dear Father God, Lover and Creator of all peoples. May we never, never, never forget all the "Natashas." In your time, in your way, we pray for your Love to be received by each Russian. Thank you in advance for each heart that is becoming yours through our efforts. Amen.

"God often asks for extraordinary obedience from people for whom He wants to do extraordinary things!"

Betty Crouse

29

ARE YOU DONE YET?

"Believe me when I say I am in the Father and the Father is in me." John 15:14

There are many reasons a parent may ask his child, "Are you done yet?" I admit I have asked the question several times during the course of a week's activities. But recently I encountered a rather startling inquiry while receiving training to spend a year doing Christian work in Estonia and Russia. The sobering question came as we were challenged to focus on our final "soul" cleansing. Our challenger presented the categories of forgiveness: broken relationships, anger, harmful gossip, and any other unresolved issues. Our task for the next few days was to complete the resolution to <u>each</u> problem, no matter what price we had to pay.

Confessions began and tears were shed as adult children called parents hundreds of miles away. Many agonized before our Lord as they stayed on their knees in deliberation until the work was done. Others surrendered everything for the first time of their spiritual journey. Some couples never slept until they both were "done" confessing and resolving long-standing differences, resentments, and just plain bitterness.

The reckoning day came as part of our final "commissioning" before we were sent out. Our personal blessing and commissiong would only come with a firm handshake and a long discerning soul-searching, eye-to-eye engagement, <u>and</u> our affirming quite assuringly, DONE! Not only did we confirm the confessional cleansing verbally, but also by penmanship by placing the word boldly and plainly on our name tag. DONE!!

What a sight to behold and an experience to enjoy as 154 commissioners walked across the platform, each giving name, origination, and country to which God had called. Only then could each declare, "YES, DR. WILKINSON, I AM DONE!!!!!" The same declaration had been made by the founder of Walk Through the Bible International spiritual leader. To be an effective laborer on a foreign soil, one must be absolutely and profoundly prayed up, confessed out, and cleansed thoroughly.

And more solidly, the provoking challenger presented, "To be one with Christ, our relationship with Him is totally dependent on our relationship with others." The perpendicular is parallel with the horizontal.

Prayer
Father, what a clarifying and thoroughly cleansing purging. Thank you for opening my eyes to another reason our earthly relationships are so critical to your plan for our lives, not to mention, effectiveness to ministry. Cleansing is so refreshing! Amen.

ONENESS

EQUALS

DONENESS

30

CAN CANDLES TALK?

"The light shines in the darkness, but the darkness has not understood it." John 1:5

Someone said to the candle, "You are giving your life away!" "Yes," answered the candle, "but what a lovely light! When my light is burning, even as small as a flicker, there are great and beautiful things that I illuminate."

The friend to the candle inquired more, "How can anything be beautiful as one is burning up?" Said the candle, "Oh, the beauty is not known by all who see me, just those who benefit from feeling my warmth and letting me safely guide them by my flicker."

A burning candle is a life well spent and used up. That is her total purpose in life. She can accomplish nothing greater.

Some candles, of course, live years in shiny brass candlesticks atop a mantel awaiting their adventure. Others are hand carved and designed to become decorative ornaments, used only as pleasing to the eye.

Candles are created from a common source. However, in order to meet her master's whims, she can be forced and molded into many sizes, colors, shapes and functions. But the candle that has fulfilled her mission is the one who has been completely and totally used up - not a single flicker of light remains. For a short time her light mattered. The candle had been created just for the day someone would say, "You are being used up by giving your life away."

As we prepared to leave the states, we made many presentations to church groups and mission circles. Simultaneously, I was packing away some of my favorite belongings. I felt myself struggling and longing to hold onto some of my "pretty, finer things" most women enjoy. I recall a conversation in a china shop when a dear friend encouraged me to take enough of "my pretty things" to feel at home on foreign shores. I pondered the statement often. "Should I or should I not?" resounded in my thoughts as I began to pack away my favorite brass candlesticks. Each of them was a special gift to me by a special friend or family member.

Then God's questions came to mind. (I'm sure the thoughts were His because they were running counter to mine). "Why not share these precious gifts you love so much with friends as a reminder to pray for you while you are away? Why not present one of your candlesticks to each mission circle who pledges prayer support?"

So as each group presentation was concluded, I presented a beautiful brass candlestick to the circle of prayer warriors and reminded them of the purpose of each candle's life. The circle leader lit the tapered white candle, and we enjoyed a precious, sweet communion in spirit. Each circle committed to lighting the candle at each circle meeting as a reminder of the light that was shining in the darkness thousands of miles away.

No sweeter peace in all the world affords the soul who has struggled with life's roles, society's boxes, demands, and performances; and after struggling finds only an empty void. Then in a sweet abandonment that only fellow strugglers can understand, she decides to give her light away - to be totally used up. Like the candle, she provides such a lovely light.

Today, I want my light to shine through _____.

Prayer

Sweet Jesus, you are the light, you are my light. Teach me to be your light. Use me up so there's not a glimmer of "me" left. Help me shine ever so brightly in the world around me. Amen.

The spent

candle's light

burns forever!

31

AN UNBROKEN VESSEL

"Search me, O God, and know my heart; test me and know my anxious thoughts. See if there is any offensive way in me, and lead me in the way everlasting." Psalm 139:23,24.

Spoiled spirits are proud people possessed, unbroken, self-sufficient spirits who desire to be served. They are driven to be recognized and are confident in how much they know.

These proud people focus on others' failures, demanding a false respect and are totally unapproachable. Their aim is to stay distant, work hard to maintain and protect their own image and reputation, and they find it difficult to share their spiritual needs with others.

Unbroken people think there's no need to repent because they have nothing of which to repent and are remorseful over their sin only when others find out.

If it sounds like I am very familiar with these surly characteristics, believe me, I am. Each of these claim familiarity with my unbroken spirit. Oh, there are many more of these piercing and self-produced traits, deep within my cracks and crevices.

God continues to perfect His love in and through me by patching and gluing the most obvious cracks. This vessel has numerous small and unnoticeable cracks to the beholder's untrained eye.

If God were looking around for a broken vessel that <u>needed</u> the most skilled potter to complete the refining process, then I know I would be chosen.

The spiritual cracks in my vessel that need the most work are _____.

Prayer

Father, whether it's a new glaze, more firing, or "shelf sitting" for a time, this broken vessel is yours. Mold or remold me as only your omnipotence can know. Whatever it takes for me to become more like you, or a vessel that can be used of you, or just more loved by you, so be it! Bring the fire on! You can trust me in your molding process. Amen.

An unbroken vessel is of little use to GOD

32

GOOD LORD, IT'S GOD!

"For I desire mercy, not sacrifice, and acknowledgment of God rather than burnt offerings." Hosea 6:6

What we believe about God determines life and all life's issues.

In *Why I Am Not A Christian* the philosopher Bertrand Russell wrote: *"God and immortality, the central dogmas of Christian religion find no support in science.... The Christian God may exist, so may the gods of Olympus, or of ancient Egypt, or of Babylon. But none of these hypotheses are more probable than any other: They lie outside the region of even probable knowledge, and therefore there is no reason to consider any of them."*

Our world is filled with confusion about God. Everyone has his own creation of who God is. And he decides, based on his imagined god, how he is going to communicate with his created image.

What we believe about God determines life for us and our daily set of activities, as well as what we think and do about other issues, even politicians. Our concept of God is a critical premise to our world view.

Whether we serve God this year on a typical "home" soil, or a foreign soil, the issue must be settled within each heart and mind: **Just who is the God to whom I am loyal and obedient and for whom I might even die?** It is crucial that we deal with God as He really is and not as we imagine Him to be.

For me, wrestling with this abstract issue began early. I spent many hours verbalizing these serious questions to our barnyard animals. As clear as if it were last week, I can mentally picture walking into the woods, through the valleys and corn fields, always resting in my own secluded respite - our pine thicket. I would audibly insist for Him "to reveal Himself to me if He were really there like the preacher had said on Sunday." Somehow, there was no connection and linking of the life I saw being lived by family each day and the God I was supposed to serve.

As my husband and I were being trained for a year of service with a different set of people who had different ideas about God, again these questions became prominent in my thinking.

If God were just being worshipped and served by me because of family tradition which has been passed down to us, my god would be an idol created to meet my need! But if God is who the Bible says He is - He is Everything! He is God! And, He is knowable. He is God!

God makes Himself knowable and believable by revealing Himself through generations of believers and non-believers, through His creation, earth, and through His most prized possession, His precious Son. How He reveals Himself is just as varied and wonderful. He is revealed in dreams and visions, seraphs and angels, through other men's voices and through His own, and then through the voice of His Son, and then through us.

Why God chooses to reveal Himself so inexhaustibly becomes clearer as our views and perceptions of Him are matched by His word, not our imaginations. What is particularly significant about God's revealing Himself most dramatically through Jesus is that it provides us with implications with which each of us must likewise reckon. Yes, what we believe about God determines life and all its issues. What we believe about Jesus determines Life with all its blessings.

If a skeptical unbeliever asks you today, "How can one really know God?" What will you say? _____.

Prayer
Father Jehovah, Yahweh, The Self Existent One, Godhead Fullness, Creative Glory and Power, Adonai, Master and Lord, we recognize your authority, power, and deity. We reverence your relationship and responsibility to us through your Son, Jesus. Amen.

You want to

be a

"know-it-all"?

Know God!

33

GOOD GOD, ITS GLORY!

"So, whatever you eat or drink or whatever you do, do it all for the glory of God."
1 Corinthians 10:31

What is the Glory of God? Paul admonished the Corinthian believers to commit even their eating and drinking...all for the Glory of God. What does this phrase mean to you on a daily basis? What does it mean to the individual paying monthly bills, relating to demanding people at work each day who truly desire to serve God day by day?

I recently was intrigued at a team bible study with these same provoking questions concerning God's Glory. Each participant gave a very different answer to the question: "How do you understand God's glory?"

Most of us think of its awesomeness because of the ambiguous way God revealed His Glory to Moses in Exodus. To see and experience God's glory and continue to sin displeases God greatly, according to another occasion God communicated with Moses. From the New Testament, we have a clear description of His Glory being "the One and Only, who came from the Father, full of grace and truth." And if the prior description is too ambiguous, let's look at Hebrews 1:3. The author states, "The Son is the radiance of God's glory, the exact representation of His being."

Back to the question: "How do these scriptures about His glory relate to you and to me on a daily basis?" When I receive bad news? When I become annoyed at my spouse's lack of attention? When I wait in line longer than twenty minutes and my patience dissipates?

In addition, how do God's purposes for each of us relate to His glory? Finally, what is God's attitude toward His own glory? Is He primarily interested and active in our daily lives to give glory away or receive?

One may ponder these inexhaustible questions of God's glory on and on and on. As we do so, let me admonish each of us to extract our perception solely on what the word of God says, not on what we feel, and not on thoughts based on abstract ideas.

A few weeks ago, I learned of my Russian neighbor's financial plight. She is such a proud woman, I feared giving her dollars or rubbles would insult her. Daily I asked God to give me wisdom and discernment in ways to help ease this precious soul's financial worries, while at the same time demonstrate His love for her in an unmistakably God-ordained way.

Immediately, numerous ways of sharing His love emerged. One way I shared His love with our team was to ask her to cook some special traditional dishes. Her clean pots and bowls were returned, running over with essential items such as flour, pasta, fruit, teas and diet sugar (she is diabetic). She accepted them graciously, although a bit reluctantly as she searched longingly deep into my eyes for real "soul" food.

In our team's discussion on how God lives His glory through us, the sharing with our neighbor was stated as a recent example and discussed by the team as the best possible answer to the session's opening question, "What is the glory of God?"

Today, I will share your Glory with _____ through _____.

Prayer

Sweet, sweet Father, Thank you for revealing to and through me, day by day experience by experience your omnipotent power and love, full of grace and truth. Amen.

G. L. O. R. Y.

GOD'S

LOVING

OMNIPOTENCE

RADIATED BY

YOU!

34

AND THAT'S THE TRUTH!

"You are near, O Lord, and all your commands are true." Psalm 119:151

Significant truths give the Bible supreme value over all other literature. Truths give Christ's body access to God's help. Someone has defined significant truth as "a single brief principle of eternal fact." Translating theology into every day life actions is not easy. These facets may help.

>Some nuggets of Significant Truth:
>* It is never contrary to God's word.
>* It is an accurate positive statement.
>* It is a fact that is binding on life and one's actions.
>* It is a clear essential element to living God's way.

To discover the significant truths the Holy Spirit has been bringing to my attention lately requires reflection and team work with the Almighty Counselor.

As we take time to pray over the truths that are revealed to us about our life and our ministry, it is essential to be open. What is the Holy Spirit impressing upon my heart, conscience or emotions? What experiences come to mind as I look at different passages? Are we able to link a truth discovered in our personal study with specific, relevant implications for our lives? Which major truths have the most bearing on situations we are facing and on our current challenges, problems, or issues?

For example, let's assume the problem my husband and I are facing is a typical ministerial challenge like, "How do I communicate with my donors back home the challenge of reaching the Estonian or Russian soul?" The Word says in Phillipians 2:30, "*...because he almost died for the work of Christ, risking his life to make up for the help you could not give me.*" **The significant truth** to my life is this: **Wholehearted devotion to Christ prompts believers to disregard their own interests in order to minister to others.**

The **implication to my life** and behavior must be to realize and welcome self-sacrifice. Such sacrifice a ministry demands for the sake of the Gospel.

Because of those Significant Truths we always have God's resources at our beckoning. **And That's The Truth!**

Today, I want to know the significance of your Word about _____ in my life!

Prayer

Father, today I ask you to help me discover truth as it relates to the situations in which I find myself, and to give me the courage to both speak and live that truth to your glory. Amen.

The Ambassador

is always

backed by the

resources of

his nation

35

TWICE THE RESURRECTION! TWICE THE JOY!

While they were still talking about this, Jesus himself stood among them and said to them, "Peace be with you." Luke 24:36

Estonian Easter services are similar to our Easter services in the States: majestic, stirring, and quite spectacular. Everyone who has the passion of gratitude in his heart sings louder and more melodiously than ever before. Those who attend the usual two services per year are just complacent and pleased with themselves for gracing the crowd with their attendance. We enjoyed the traditional service very much.

Russian Orthodox services are traditionally held the Sunday after the Western Evangelical Easter services are celebrated. The difference in the schedules allowed us to accept our next door neighbor's invitation to attend Easter worship services with her. We had accepted with honor and gratitude to be able to share this special worship time with such a special lady, the one I have affectionately referred to in some earlier writings as "MeeMaw."

The sanctuary was beginning to be quite crowded as we arrived around ten in the morning. MeeMaw took us to the different saints, explained quietly the significance of each, lit her candle in reverence to each Patriarch of the Russian Orthodox religion and hailed Mary accordingly.

When she returned from spending time with the priest, her eyes showed tears of a burdensome nature. I wondered if she were crying tears of sadness over the ongoing **hostile dispute between the Estonian Orthodox Church and the Russian Orthodox Church.** Seemingly, the dispute is over who owns all the splendid interior in the Russian Orthodox Church, or according to MeeMaw, "what little is left of it." Simply put, Estonian leaders who are currently in control seem to believe they also own everything inside their former tyrant's worship houses. And maybe they do. And just maybe the current strife had absolutely nothing to do with those tears MeeMaw wiped away as she returned to continue our worship, all six hours, all standing.

As we quietly moved around the sanctuary at MeeMaw's leading and marveled at thousands who came to kiss their saints, we realized that these saints were church political figures and not biblical saints. (There is even a St. George, but to my surprise there is no St. Sharon).

MeeMaw noticed with concern my tears as I watched in dismay and much sadness. My becoming moved to tears led MeeMaw to ask if we wanted to leave in time to attend our worship service. We assured her we were enjoying ourselves. She had misread my weeping!

As the mood grew somber, and still in her very broken and limited English, MeeMaw began to share deep spiritual needs and concerns she had for herself, her daughter, and her teenage grandson. For several minutes I felt the precious Counselor, the Holy Spirit, hovering over us. MeeMaw exerted much energy and effort to find the appropriate English words. There was never a question about her message to us. It was quite gloriously clear. She knew we had communicated; the receiver had received the message the sender had intended. **MeeMaw had asked me to spend some time with her touring, "just the two of us," around the city to do "deep heart talk, talk woman to woman about God and Spirit and ...."** Then she asked George to please talk to her wayward grandson whom we had met and been with several times. She expressed a burden she had for him to know George's God.

Humbled and stunned, George and I knew God was indeed being worshipped on their Easter Sunday. Since moving in, we had both believed there was His special reason for our immediate bond and friendship with MeeMaw and her grandson. Even with being away from our home church to worship our Risen Savior, we had been wonderfully blessed twice this holy Season, and twice asked to share His love.

A few hours later the Sunday bus was less crowded than its usual state. MeeMaw, George and I scurried to trolley # 6 to catch a ride home where, George and I would grab our luggage to take a taxi to the bus station by twelve noon. We were due in Latvia, a sister Baltic state, by sundown!

MeeMaw was delighted in getting to enlighten us more about the area when the trolley breaks jammed to a sudden, jolting stop. MeeMaw barreled into the Plexiglas petition which separates the driver from the occupants of the bus. Two men, each weighing over 200 pounds were hurled in on top of MeeMaw, who had tumbled down into the steps by the front door.

Everyone seemed to be shocked into a state of total stillness until George and I **realized <u>we</u> had to help MeeMaw**. We feared a broken neck, knees, back, or at least a broken nose because she had plummeted face forward into the petition. As we, fearing the worst, carefully laid her back onto the seats, the trolley operator took the long connectors away from the wiring so that the trolley couldn't move. This ignited a fiery uproar from a load of angry trolley passengers who had no choice but to find another mode of transportation. I'm certain we were being cursed black and blue, but since we couldn't understand "nary a word," it didn't hurt "nary a bit." We just smiled and said, "Do you speak English? We do not understand." They stomped their feet, shook their fist, and left murmuring very loudly.

Soon the doctors and police were all around us. Immediately the police began checking passports. Quietly, I whispered down in MeeMaw's ear I had stupidly left mine at home, first time ever. Quickly she shared with the officials we were close friends of hers visiting from America. My passport was never requested. George's was.

In all her misery MeeMaw kept trying to say, "Bussijaam," "go! go! go!" George finally told her she might as well save her breath for I was as stubborn as she was. MeeMaw tried to smile but couldn't. We were asked to accompany MeeMaw home in the ambulance so they could check her again for shock and heart. The young doctor was very gentlemanly, watching over us even as he took care of our friend.

Soon we had called her daughter, bid farewell to the doctor, and kissed the forehead of our dear, sweet, next-door neighbor, MeeMaw. Hurriedly we taxied to the bus station and climbed into a moving bus. As I settled down trying to soak in all that had happened and thinking of MeeMaw's deep spiritual quest in the morning worship service, I wondered if Satan was so scared of MeeMaw's total understanding of what Easter is really all about that he tried to destroy her. I do not fully understand the Eastern Orthodox Religion and, perhaps, never will. But a religion without Christ's resurrection is a people without a hope. People **without a hope** are seeking the REAL hope, and the only Real Hope is Jesus, the true Saint to kiss.

Truly, we have experienced the Resurrection twice this year in Tallinn, Estonia. And, truly we have experienced twice the joy! And truly we look forward with great anticipation to the great day we are privileged to kiss Jesus Christ, the true and living Son of God, (In reverence and awe).

Prayer

Father, Lord of all, we thank you for such an awesome experience as worshipping you in a foreign culture, in a foreign way. Would you show your grace to MeeMaw and grant her your real and personal joy, your son Jesus Christ. Amen.

Gentle stillness

comes often in

a whisper of

understanding

36

UNSEEN PRESENCE

"He replied, 'My mother and brothers are those who hear God's words and put it into practice.'"
Luke 8:21

Oh God, if I had known it were you, I would have given my very best! It was just a raggedy, torn, smeared and smudged cookbook - - my favorite one. My translator, a dear Russian young lady, far away from her home of origin, Moscow, seemed terribly lonely. For some strange reason, I sensed an instant pull to become friends. Almost immediately she responded. As we discussed exchanging Russian and American recipes, I remembered the well-used cookbook back at my flat, hardly still in one piece.

I brought the cookbook to the next language class and shared with Svettie, the pet name we gave our translator. After the agreed-upon week of copying recipes, she admitted she was keeping it longer because she was trying to rewrite all the recipes. She explained how much her husband of four months loved for her to cook and try new recipes. She enjoyed pleasing him.

A great yearning of compassion came over me as I accepted the returned and still-ragged cookbook. Without even processing the thought, I turned and penned my best wishes and signed, "your new American friend, always and forever." A teary eyed Svettie accepted the gift and hugged it close to her breast. Days later she shared that it was "the most special of anything anyone had done for her since arriving in the country all alone a few months earlier." She cried as she told of the pain as she left her mother and family to make her nest in her new homeland of her husband, Estonia. I could see her heart pounding as she talked of her feelings of alienation, not understanding the language, being misinterpreted, ignored, and even discriminated against by the Estonians who seem to hate any Russian. She explained how her own family didn't seem to understand fully of her decision to leave her mother homeland.

    A few weeks later as I tried in vain to prepare a dish without the usual accompaniment of the raggedy recipe book, I began to regret so thoughtlessly handing over my dear companion to an almost stranger. Then a strange, <u>unseen presence</u> entered our cozy little kitchen. A kind and gentle voice asked me a startling question: "Oh troubled one, **if the receiver of your gift had been <u>me</u>, what would you have done?**" Without hesitating I responded, "Oh Father, of course if I had known it were you, I would have given my very best." My own words haunted me for days as I pondered the question of this unseen presence.

    A few weeks later we were invited as <u>honored</u> guests to help Svettie celebrate her birthday in the traditional Russian custom. In addition to the expected flowers and chocolates, I watched carefully as she opened my special gift to her...another cookbook, but this time it was a <u>brand</u> <u>new</u>, <u>never</u> <u>used</u>, <u>potato cookbook</u>!!

    Today, I will share my very best _____ _____ with my friend _____.

Prayer
Oh Father, help me, as I live and work around many opportunities to share your love through me, to be aware that they deserve the very best from me. Amen.

Refuse to give

to God that

which costs

you nothing!

Betty Crouse

37

MIDNIGHT TRAIN TO MOSCOW

"My Father, if it is possible may this cup be taken from me. Yet not as I will but as you will."
Matthew 26:39

We were scheduled to cross the Estonian and Russian border precisely at midnight as part of this sixteen-hour train ride to Moscow. A brief orientation had been given to prepare us for the methodical and somewhat alarming experience. Three different groups of armed officials would arrive, knock on our compartment and demand to check our visas, passports, declaration report and to search our luggage. "Merely routine. Do not be alarmed. Do as they ask. You have nothing to hide," we were instructed as we arrived at our assigned compartment. Since it was George's and my very first train ride of this nature, we touched, examined and enjoyed everything in the compartment, exhibiting a ten-year-old's excitement. We stared for hours at the countryside that was still covered fully by layers of old and newly fallen snow. Everything was beautiful and mysterious.

Precisely at midnight, just as we were told, the old, but comfortable train arrived at the border. Almost immediately, pounding began on our compartment door. Visas and declaration reports were examined and approved by the first group to appear.

The second group came almost immediately and asked for our passports. Suddenly and curiously, the armed soldier began to instruct us rather hastily to get our things, prepare to leave the train, and go with him to the station. "We arrest you," he stated.

When we reunited our bottom jawbone with the top one, George turned to me and said, "Get our luggage together. They are arresting us." "Why? What have we done? I'm not leaving this train. It is dark outside. We don't know how far it is to the police station...." Panicky, George again instructed me to prepare to leave the train because we had no choice. As I made my way to the compartment door, I prayed a simple but mindful prayerful plea to our God of refuge. "You said, nothing will harm us, so now is your chance to prove it, Father. Cause if you don't we're about to land in a jail where no one speaks English. Please protect us." I asked the officer to explain to me again what the problem was because I did not understand. The story was changing a bit each time of the many times we pretended not to understand.

At first, our passport had been violated. Supposedly, we had stayed in Estonia longer than the allotted time of one month. Not true - allotted time was three months - Next explanation was added a tell-tell feature we had not heard of before - we must pay 1000 Krooni or $100 U.S. dollars.

Desperately, I reached in my documents and pulled out a list of our Russian and Estonian translators and showed it to the officer and amazingly, authoritatively declared, "I am not leaving the train until I can speak to one of our interpreters. I do not understand." What I did not understand was "Why?" we were being arrested and escorted off the train.

The officer left and returned shortly with his superior, a more rigid and stern-looking officer who also carried large guns. He looked mad and mean. Nevertheless, determined the only way

I was leaving my safe, well lighted compartment was on my heels and hinney, I continued to pretend not to understand.

At least an hour of discussion continued. We're told again we must pay 1000 Krooni - We told him we would love to if we had it but we just didn't have any money except what we declared. Without any further ado, the supervisor ordered the officer to stamp the passports. As the officer obeyed, we pledged our thanks and gratitude to show reverence and respect.

George and I embraced as we breathed a huge sigh of relief. We then bowed and shared a thanksgiving prayer of reverence and respect to our Superior Officer - the Officer we want to have with us each time we make this **Midnight Train Ride To Moscow.**

Father, Superior Officer, sometimes I forget to include you in _____.

Prayer
Sweet, Sweet, Jesus, Thank you for your complete protection. When we are totally dependent upon you, you show your grace once again. Will you ride with us back home, too? Amen.

God Plus

One

is Always

A Majority

38

HIS DOUBLE PLEASURE

"But when you give to the needy do not let your left hand know what your right hand is doing, so that your giving may be in secret." Matthew 6:3

As we left our home in Tallinn, the sun was shining brilliantly in a soft blue sky. On the outskirts of town, snow began to spit to and fro horizontally. The countryside was magnificently trimmed with the still of several inches of packed snowflakes. I sensed we were in for a beautiful three days in rural Estonia.

Upon arrival at the town's junior high school, painted a pastel pink, we noted many similarities between their town's school and our U.S. rural schools.

After ministry and teaching in the school, our interpreter Bob led us to a small dilapidated flat. I was forewarned about the flat's bathrooms, but not enough. The rust had eroded every part of the bathroom's equipment. So much so that the rusted lever inside a topless commode must be pulled to flush. The tub and lavatory were in the same pathetically run-down condition.

But I noticed there was no dirt, filth, or uncleanness, just old worn out things. Also, I noticed a strong pride of family as I admired photographs displayed proudly in the glass bookcase.

Books seemed to be their second love, as is true with most Estonian and Russian people.

After enjoying a homemade American-like pizza, the lovely lady I shall call Mary, who neither spoke nor understood a word of English, took down her personal scrapbook for us to peruse. For fifteen years this still beautiful, striking, elderly pensioner had been a successful actress of the Russian theater. Her scrapbook was filled with snapshots of her numerous roles, usually portraying a beautiful vixen. I sensed such kindness and sadness from her eyes and hands. I wasn't certain why.

Later that evening, I learned through our translator that in order to have enough beds for us, the husband, wife and son (a high school senior), would take a 9 P.M. bus several miles out to their ten-acre farmhouse to sleep for the night, returning in the early A.M.

My complete understanding of their babbling came too late to stop them from going. I was embarrassed, humbled, sad, and uncomfortable. Why would they give up their bed and their home to strangers about whom they knew nothing? More than that, why would they inconvenience themselves to make us feel special?

We were given their bedroom, filled with their older son's typical collection of musical groups, cars, coke cans, etc. One complete wall was filled with high school ribbons of honor and awards for academia. I learned the next morning that this precious son had been killed two years earlier in an automobile accident.

The husband was the one who returned early the next morning. We will call him Joseph. We invited him to join us for breakfast in a nearby cafe. Hurriedly, Joseph grabbed his "Sunday best" suit, fur hat, and topcoat. He had a sparkle almost childlike in his Finnish, blue eyes. His sense of pride was evidenced by his proudly responding when, through our interpreter, I asked if he would be so kind as to escort me to breakfast. Outside, the snow was falling furiously as we explored the quaint shops in this picturesque village in Southern Estonia.

After breakfast he insisted he help carry our luggage as we strolled slowly several blocks awaiting our bus departure. As we bid our farewells of gratitude and thanksgiving for such unforgettable hospitality, I formed a mental picture of Joseph and Mary, his bride of many years, giving up their own bedroom in their warm home and traveling afar to their "back stable," a cold farmhouse, to make room for two strangers, with no strings attached, nothing in return.

As our "milk stop" bus ride of five hours finally reentered the outskirts of our home city, Tallinn, I sensed God's pleasure with our visit to Voru. Glancing over to the right I saw a sunset mysteriously present the glorious sun and a shadow of the sun, each as significant and beautiful as the other.

For some reason, known only to Him, reflecting on the events of the visit to Voru, I sensed His double pleasure awesomely demonstrated by His double sunset. I was humbled as I recalled Jesus' loving reminder, "In as much as you have done it unto one of the least of these, my brethren, you have done it unto me."

Today, I sense God's double pleasure when I _____
_____.

Prayer
Thank you gracious God for each of your pleasures. Thank you especially when we sense your double pleasures. Amen.

God's person

in God's place,

at God's work,

in God's way,

will never lack

God's supply

39

MAMA, CORNBREAD, BUTTER AND ME

"Honor your father and your mother, so that you may live long in the land the Lord your God is giving you." Exodus 20:12

What is your very first memory of your most important relationship? For me it was five years of age.

My mother was always my haven of safety. She was my fortress against a big cruel world for a five-year-old girl, the seventh of eight children. There was not time in the late 40s for a farmer's wife to spend adequate time with each of the children. If she did, it might mean meals for the entire family would not be ready and available at the expected time.

One chore I recall fondly. I was expected to help Mama with the churning of fresh butter. I didn't understand how the wooden churn worked to produce a soft, solid mass from a thin bumpy liquid, but Mama did. Once the clabbered milk had turned to the desired consistency, Mama and I removed the butter and placed it in a rectangle, wooden mold for hardening.

Today, my thoughtful Mama had made a new skillet full of cornbread that was smelling mighty fine when she removed it piping hot from the oven, exactly the time the butter had completed its cycle. I can smell the indescribably delicious smell of the freshly-made cornbread as if it were yesterday. No other brothers and sisters were around that special day for some wonderful reason. Just Mama and I feasted on the absolutely perfect lunch that warm, fall day. Steak and potatoes would have been not one bit better!

Yesterday, a care package came from a wonderful lady whom I have never met. She joined our Sunday School class after our leaving for Estonia. Among many other wonderful needed items were two packages of self-rising corn meal. It was very special as we had seen none since entering this non-corn producing country. We had attempted several times to get help to find it in the local grocery stores, but there was no Estonian word in which to translate the word "corn."

I made the cornbread in a flash. The only dried beans I had found were being saved for this occasion - beans, cornbread, and milk, one of my favorite childhood meals. I took out Estonia's internationally mentioned butter (VOIX) and spread across the top of the most beautiful slice of cornbread the world has ever seen (at least from my perspective).

The fragrances and all the beautiful memories of that <u>one</u> special time my Mama and I had shared fresh butter and fresh cornbread came flooding into my mind. I sat for a long time reminiscing that and other special times this memory had provoked. Thanks to a wonderful friend I've still not met, many memories continued all day – memories of a wonderful time in my life when it was just **Mama, Cornbread, Butter and Me.**

My favorite fragrance of home is _____.

Prayer

Thank you, Sweet Father, for giving us the sense of smell and of memory. Thank you for my mother and each memory I have of her goodness and kindness and special attention to me. Amen.

We get

experiences

by having

experiences!

40

ODE TO TOBY
OUR TRUSTED FRIEND

"So in everything, do to others what you would have them do to you, for this sums up the Law and the Prophets." Matthew 7:12

When our nineteen-year-old son, Blaine, was very ill with acute leukemia, he was often asked to share his wishes and dreams with friends. One day I overheard him tell one of our friends he would love to have a yellow Labrador Retriever.

After several unsuccessful attempts to talk my husband into assisting me to help our son have one of his wishes, I gave up on the idea. I knew he was right about our garden home being too small. I forgot about the idea, for then. A few years later, the week we moved into a larger, old country-style home with large yards and pastures, the idea came back. Why not have our precious son, whom God had healed from leukemia, a yellow lab for his Christmas? We both agreed.

Blaine had graduated college and was awarded a Fulbright Scholar's Award to Dangreiga, Belize, Central America. My mother's intuition told me the dog would be good for him to feel connected to home. My boy was a long way from his roots.

This time I could not be talked out of it. It was all planned. So I began to scheme. Even a dear friend chided in and agreed to house our newly purchased animal "Toby" for a few weeks until Blaine arrived home for Christmas. On Christmas Eve, Toby was delivered with red kerchief and Christmas ribbon, and a Christmas card dangling from his neck. It was love at first sight. From that moment on I seemed to be second place in my son's heart. Toby always came first.

For the first few months, the family questioned my reasoning abilities in finding a dog for which to care while Blaine completed eighteen months in another country. Even Blaine found it inconceivable and as he put it, "not well thought out." I was reminded every long distance phone conversation. Each began and ended with questions and discussions about his best friend, Toby.

Even George became attached as he attempted to care for the adventurous mut. We spent many hours searching in our neighborhood for Toby as a result of his breaking his chain. He even lunged headlong into a moving vehicle that knocked him cold just because he could. There was never a dog like our Toby!!! That's for certain. Even the local animal shelter knew us and Toby on a first-name basis. We frequented the shelter all too often to procure this loving and crazy lab.

As a last resort, George and Toby entered obedience school and graduated with honors. At least George did! He received the "most improved" master award. Toby got honorable mentions. Time flew by and Blaine completed his work in Belize. Fondly, all of us played with Toby and adored this new-found, family friend. Because of his growing esteemed place of respect in our family's heart, he became affectionately known as Mr. Toby.

When Blaine settled in his Arkansas apartment to continue his course work on his graduate degree, a birthday gift was delivered from our home in Alabama. You guessed it. It was Mr. Toby. With the same red kerchief, ribbon, and a birthday card, the bouncing eighty-pounder (this time wearing red plastic sunglasses) jumped into his best friend's arms. It was truly a moving sight to behold. Tears welled up as I breathed one of my many prayers thanking God for the insight years ago to provide a wish to my son.

After battling with Toby through a spell of heartworms, Blaine remarked to me that he believed it was meant for him and Toby to be together. When I questioned why, he soberly stated, "We both seem to have an awful lot of bad luck. I just think we belong together." I smiled. I thought so, too!

As our son called home from school, he always updated us on Toby's adjusting to his new Arkansas home and neighbors. It wasn't long until I could hear Toby breathing while we were talking. Blaine explained that Toby had edged his way in from the screened front porch inch by inch, night by night until, finally, he was inside, sleeping beside Blaine's bed. Later conversations revealed Toby was sleeping closer than beside the bed.

As Blaine's degree work was completed and job offers began to present themselves, many were not considered because of Blaine's traveling companion and housemate, Mr. Toby. I began to understand more of the closeness of this beautiful and precious friendship.

Finally, the perfect position was decided upon. Mr. Toby and Blaine packed up all their belongings and arrived in Tallulah, Louisiana. They were employed to be part of a research team for the National Wildlife Reserve. Days would be spent out in the forest, with the team, birds, and, of course, researcher Toby. The entire team viewed Toby as an integral team member. Of course his master was proud and his constant companion and career critter, Toby, was as pleased as punch. George and I missed them both very much, but gained much consolation in knowing the two were together, always. After all, they belonged together. We were certain either would give his life in protection of the other. What friends! What devotion! Could God have had this kind of relationship in mind when He created man and animals?

Soon, my husband and I departed for our new adventure to serve as Christian workers in the country of Estonia. We left with many pictures of family, friends, and, yes, Mr. Toby too. We knew our son would be fine. After all, he had with him everyday Almighty God who had healed him from leukemia, and Mr. Toby, who had healed him from loneliness.

Not long after arriving in Estonia, I began to have a gnawing feeling regularly that our son would really be lost without what seemed to be at this point his soulmate for life, Toby. A few times I even mentioned it to George. And of course, we both would change the subject lest we miss the both of them too much.

A few weeks after that first gnawing dread, the phone rang with a call from half way around the globe. It was our grieving son, sobbing so we could not make out his words at first. We finally pieced together his scattered fragments of words and realized he had just two hours earlier buried Toby. Apparently, Toby had gotten too hot while taking his daily exercise run and died after collapsing with a seizure. Blaine was devastated. So were we. Our family had just suffered a tremendous loss. Our loved one carried with him a great chunk of all our hearts.

A few days later we called our son for a longer time of consolation. He was trying to describe just what Toby had meant to him. Toby was his companion, his pal, his co-researcher, his exercise partner. They had been together practically every day for the past four years. He would never find another friend like Toby, he said.

Never before had I understood the meaning of a dog being man's best friend. But my son, Blaine, and Mr. Toby epitomized that saying.

Today I want to thank you for my most trusted friend
_____.

Prayer
Thank you, Lord, for the discernment to help my son find his most trusted friend, Toby. Thank you for the joy their friendship brought to our lives. Thank you for using a family pet to draw our family closer. And, thank you for the intuition you've given me lately for a wonderful Christmas present for our son this year. Ummm......, a red ribbon, a large, red Christmas bow, and.... Perhaps a Merry Christmas wish from our Trusted Friend. Amen.

Satisfaction comes when we are content, regardless

41

NAGAMASINI JA TERE HUMMIKUST!

GOODBYE AND HELLO

"I am the Alpha and the Omega, the First and the Last, the Beginning and the End."
Revelation 22:13

As George and I worshipped with Robert Schuller's Hour of Power last Sunday morning, I was intrigued with the title and concept of his message, "Good-bye and Hello."

Dr. Schuller stated that the inverted order of Good-bye and Hello was indeed no mistake. It was well intended! He carefully carried us through our stages of life and encouraged us to reminisce of our good-byes and hellos we had encountered in our own lifetimes. I never moved beyond this current year, 1996, location, Estonia.

It seems much of our daily routine here is embroidered with good-byes and hellos. New acquaintances and encounters happen several times each day. The Estonian names are difficult to spell and pronounce, much less remember. Another part of our life here is one of serving as hosts to American visitors, mostly here on CoMission business. Several times a year we say "good-bye" to often newly made friends and "hello" to those just arriving.

Often as we minister around the country, we make special friends who are close to our hearts. Estonians call such persons "heart friends." I like that! Good-byes to heart friends are sweet sorrows. Robert Schuller reminded us each good-bye was set up by our Lord to better prepare us for a grand hello to our next friend.

Several good-byes have had major impact on George and me this year. In April, five members of our team who had arrived in July of 1995 had to return to the states. Their recall by God to serve another year in Estonia mandated they raise another year of funding. These five individuals were a very special part of our new-found family here in Estonia. It was definitely a sweet sorrow. Even with our knowing if God willed they would return, we still grieved as we said our good-byes at the airport.

Busyness in preparing to say "hello" to the Frazer college youth team helped relieve our grief. Before long we were greeting with grand hellos and kisses on each beautiful and tired face of our precious Frazer family. The ten days we experienced their overflow of tender love and affection gave a new meaning to George and me for the term, Tender Loving Care. Our sweet sorrow good-byes to the Frazer dozen left a "chocolate chip" fragrance for us to enjoy for a very long time.

In the midst of Frazer's ministry tour here, three members of our team, the remainder of the 1995 cycle, had ended their year of ministry and were due to fly out on July 3rd. Even though we felt torn with leaving Frazer's team for several hours, all of our team except the youth project coordinator spent several hours traveling back to Tallinn's airport to bid another Grand Good-bye. Even though much time and effort had been spent in the closing weeks to shower these departing three with lots of love, love,

love, none of us were prepared for the sweet, sweet sorrow shared at this departure. Three very special "heart friends" were leaving our family and heading off to Oregon and Canada. For these special ones, only God knows if we will have a grand hello on this earth.

Now, as I sit writing this, our team's schedule is becoming quite hectic and very busy preparing for our Grand Hello to the 1995 team members who all were refunded (praise the Lord). We even picked up a new comer to join our team and family. This part of our family will be arriving next week. What a Grand Hello we shall experience!!!

But a different good-bye for this team is just around the corner. This week we have received e-mails from our supervisors working out the logistics of our team re-entering the U.S. The Lord willing, Mary and Karmelle are returning for another year in Estonia. Denise is returning to the states anticipating a 1997 wedding.

After many good-byes are said, George and I are planning, unless God directs otherwise, to experience the Grandest Hello of our lifetime to our dear, precious friends and family.

Yes, I do agree with Dr. Schuller who said, "Every good-bye is an upward movement."

I will soon be saying goodbye to _____.

Prayer

Father, thank you for each goodbye and each hello you have provided to us. Each friend and each stranger has touched our lives, and left us with purpose. Amen.

God's timing is none of our business -- our response is.

42

MY LOVE CLOSET

"Not only so, but we also rejoice in our sufferings, because we know that suffering produces perseverance; perseverance, character; and character, hope." Romans 5:3

When we entered our four-room flat, I gasped from shock. The walls had been clawed by large dogs. The first few days I just walked around and looked at the holes and unattractive markings.

The water closet was in a separate room from our toilet. The toilet was the room I liked the least. It was so small that if George at 6'8" decided to sit down, his knees came out into the entrance area. The door would not close, much less lock.

I decided to try the decorating trick of disillusioning the eye. I gathered the few hello cards received from friends from the states and taped them on the ugly, school-house green walls. As other cards came in, I taped them each on the walls, all of which were only a few inches from my eyes' view.

I gained much strength from the enjoyment of reading and rereading the notes of encouragement, written prayers, and mission-circle cards with every member's well wishes. I began to pray for each of these precious friends who took time from their hectic schedules. It became a special time for me to be reminded to pray for each of our well wishers. As the cards and notes continued to come in, each was placed in a special place in my "Love Closet."

One dear friend sent cartoons cut from local newspapers. The walls surrounding the toilet, within reach while sitting, were saved for cartoons. We placed a glass of colored markers on the floor and a note taped to the cover of the scratched and ugly tissue cover. The note read, "While you sit, nothing to do and see, how about coloring cartoons for me." Today, most of the cartoons are colored. Often during a team meeting at our flat, a team member will go missing for quite a while. Later we see another cartoon colored and initialed.

Another friend sent two pink balloons and said, "Have a happy day." We did after I tied the balloons up on the ceiling of the lovely room.

In the scriptures Jesus tells us to go into a closet when we pray and that what we pray in secret will be rewarded openly. What a blessing to have the privilege of praying daily for <u>each</u> caring friend, some of whom I have yet to meet. What a privilege to serve in a foreign land a Loving God who can turn a shabby toilet into my favorite room in my home -- my Love Closet.

Today, I will claim _____ room in my house as my Love Closet.

Prayer
Lord God, forgive me for not thinking of my closet as a place to hide away and to love you, even more. Amen.

Jesus loves

"Come as you are"

prayer meetings!

43

EVERYDAY MAINTENANCE

"If you then, though you are evil, know how to give good gifts to your children, how much more will your Father in heaven give the Holy Spirit to those who ask him!" Luke 11:13

One of the great lessons God has been teaching George and me this year is His ever presence. Each day He has manifested Himself. So boldly evident is His care for providing mundane, everyday details of our life needs. This everyday maintenance plan is totally consistent, following with us everywhere we go or stay, every night or day, in all we do or do not say.

Recently, our ornithologist (bird researcher) son, Blaine, spent a few days with us worshipping with our team in a Russian Methodist church. He experienced our everyday work world of team meetings, Spiritual Life, and Bible studies. My requested prayer had been for God to reveal Himself to all of us, especially to our son, that he would get a real good glimpse of not just the God of his created friends, but the God of every little detail of our lives.

The next few days of travel we experienced some quirky, challenging, and unique experiences. See what you think about this amazing key concept and principle we're experiencing in a special way this year: GOD is involved in every detail!

We had found two world renowned bird sanctuaries for Blaine to visit. The travel agent (the only one who could speak English) told us which busses to take to get the taxi to the town where the bird sanctuaries are.

Of course, as with everything else here, it was incorrect information and caused us to get off the bus in the wrong town where no one spoke English. After several minutes and no progress with the ticket clerk at the bus station, I went out to the town, found a young teen (more of them at least understand English) and asked her what to do. She advised us to go with her on her bus to a small town. **Then about that time a taxi pulled up which the ticket agent had called for us (without our asking).** The driver was a Russian, and we were in an Estonian community!!!

We explained and showed words in writing. He told us how much it would cost for him to take us to the bird museum on the sanctuary. We got in and drove several miles to what he thought was the place - But, guess what! It was not. He walked to nearby houses to ask where the museum was and they directed us to another narrow, dirt road several miles away. He stopped at a house with a thatched reed roof, built in the 1700's. There he found two ladies from Finland (this is their summer house where they grow vegetables). They actually spoke and understood English. Guess what? **They were also bird watchers who had chosen the summer cottage just for that purpose.** Coincidence, I think not! Neither did Blaine. Our taxi driver looked amused!

They shared bird information with our *Birdbrain Blaine* and gave us maps to get to the sanctuary (a small amount of land and a large amount of birds). All this time the **Russian taxi driver named Peter (who was now on a first name basis)** was leaning against the taxi and was totally amused! I got pictures of everyone, the old homestead, and off we went down a narrow, dirt road with a Russian who knew our survival depended on him. Scary thought? There was total peace!

Well, a while later we got to the bird place, and Blaine went off with binoculars and bird book. George, Peter and I opened the taxi trunk and ate our lunch. (I learned the first week never to go anywhere without food and water). So we had cheese (hunks), bread (not sliced), cookies our neighbor had made for Blaine's arrival, and water. It was wonderful!!

After three hours of walking around and waiting, we got back in the taxi with Peter and proceeded to the ferry - many miles away. You may think, why not catch a bus, it would be cheaper. We thought the same and found out NO buses this far out! But Peter was a gentle business man, and we made an all day deal which turned him into a tour guide/taxi driver. Of course Blaine was footing this bill, and he said that finding many new bird species to add to his list made the taxi and tour guide fare of $50 per day seem reasonable.

Later - AT THE FERRY ON AN ISLAND CALLED SAAREMAA. Blaine was heaving like his best canine friend Toby used to do when he retrieved sticks from the water. He could smell the birds! I could only smell dust and fish! I wished I could smell coffee!

Peter got out at the ferry crossing, got all the information that would tell us the time the ferry would leave -- which was immediately! We ran to get on the ferry and off we went. He kept yelling 3:10 and pointing to his watch. Whatever happens at 3:10 must be important. It was then 2:30 P.M.

We found ourselves a spot to stand outside in open air on the ferry - the only place to stand. We rode for forty-five minutes across the ferocious Baltic Sea to the island. It was great fun and perfect weather! We got out more cheese and bologna and crackers and had our own little picnic on top of some tarpaulins. Everyone looked at us like we were crazy, <u>but</u> they do that in the states! Wonder why? So, we got off the ferry on the other side to try and purchase 3:10 bus tickets to the town where we could get another taxi to get to the bird sanctuary #2. <u>Except</u>, **there was no 3:10 bus. We had a four-hour wait.**

So, we broke out a new loaf of bread (now you know why I'm gaining weight don't you?), found a table and chairs to rest for a few minutes while Blaine looked for new birds along the seashore! Then we got smart after a cup of coffee that would put any brain to perking! If a bus came on the next ferry, we would try to catch it and purchase our ticket on the bus! We all agreed that would beat waiting for four hours and would put us in the next town around 9 P.M. The travel agent back in Tallinn said all hotels were full and we had to call a farm house (bed and breakfast) 6 kilometers out of town. That seemed fine to us. We were prepared to sleep in the bus station (if they had one). Worse case scenario was to ride back and forth on top of tarpaulins on the ferry all night long for a few dollars each way. Okay. So, we asked four different ferry-crossing personnel how to catch the bus should it be on the next ferry. We got four different answers.

We decided on our own procedure, like "thumbing" with bags on our backs directly in the middle of the road where the bus <u>must</u> stop - It worked! There was a bus - which had some seats - and after several minutes we were allowed on! Hallelujah! We were on our way to Kurasaare. Around 7 P.M. we were getting really tired! I opened my eyes once to see the surrounding area, and at the front of the bus hung a huge, bold clock which read - you guessed it: 3:10. But the actual time was much later. I pointed out the clock to my husband and son. We all laughed heartily and applauded and shook our heads as we marveled.

Once we arrived, we developed a plan of action to find a bed (remember we were told there were none). We decided to find an information center (like there was one). Another surprise; there was one! The first call had us a room in the center of town. A very good place, good restaurant, and good price. Thank you Lord! We ate the rest of the food in our pack.

The next morning, I was too exhausted to move. I convinced George and Blaine to find this bird sanctuary on a joining island without me. They agreed and left me lying in bed at 5:30 A.M. Imagine that! What kind of raising did I have to sleep so late? Well, a few hours later I was downstairs taking advantage of any protein their free breakfast might offer and chatting with some Americans from New York (former Estonians). I turned to get my coffee cup and there stood my two men. They had been to the end of the island only to find out there was only transportation out to the bird sanctuary #2 every other day, and guess what? This was not the day! Someone forgot to tell us that part!

Blaine took his bird book and binoculars and headed for the town's coastline where he sighted more new finds for his professional records. George and I toured an old castle, walked in the park, chatted with some art students from Finland, and just had a lovely morning. At 2 P.M. we all gathered at the bus station, got some food from a small grocery store, and yes you guessed it, we got a loaf of bread, ham, cheese and this time we found a coke and an Estonian ice cream bar! Heaven!!

We hoped we had been sold the proper bus tickets for the correct bus route back to Tallinn where we were scheduled to leave for St. Petersburg, Russia at 10 P.M. by train the next evening. We made it home, but only after an hour's delay to change a tire that blew out on the rough road we were traveling. The blow out was a blessing in disguise for me and my small bladder. Busses with <u>no</u> bathrooms can be a problem for us "sb" people. But while the flat was being changed, George, Blaine and I found a beautiful, all natural bathroom - one more detail our Logistics Expert and constant Traveling Companion provided.

We discussed all the many details that were provided us on this two-day adventure and then thanked the God of our universe for being our God of personal details and everyday things!

Today, I want to thank you for _____.

Prayer
Thank you, Sweet Jesus, for being our personal tour guide, protector, communicator, and roadway today. We needed you to show up. You did and we are glad. Amen.

Peaceful People

are

Powerful People

44

HAVE YOU EVER THANKED GOD FOR BROWN SUGAR?

"And my God will meet all your needs according to his glorious riches in Christ Jesus."
Philippians 4:19

After searching for food for weeks, the five members of our Estonian ministry team decided to take the challenge and compete with each other in our search for brown sugar. Besides that, we were all craving chocolate chip cookies. So, as we walked to busses, trolleys, trains and ministry appointments we passed numerous "kiosks" or prefab-like, small storage buildings turned into stores. Each one passed could be housing our precious find, brown sugar.

Most grocery stores had been thoroughly checked while searching for other needed items such as baggies, Pam cooking spray, aluminum foil, cinnamon, vinegar, and soft toilet paper. You see, the problem for us is <u>not</u> that most foods don't exist in this large city. Estonia has more commercial goods to offer her citizenry each and every day. She is beginning to take on a real European look.

The problem for us is that we are not accustomed to their supply and demand system - especially when it comes to anything beyond daily staples necessary to sustain us. Most weeks we spend several hours walking, looking for specific food items. But where to find them is anyone's guess.

For example, there might be a supply of women's underwear displayed next to a set of automobile tires and hardware tools. The most frustrating part of this puzzle is that once we find the longed-for item in a certain store, we never expect to find it there again.

When in the states, we never realized how much routine there was in where we bought the things until, suddenly, there was no routine. One Saturday morning George and I decided to experience our first McDonald's since arriving in Estonia. It was about three miles away. As we walked past a Statoil Service Station, we decided it smart for us to peruse the shelves for any needed items. Of course, we were well-supplied with our most critical pocketed item -- plastic bags. Over here there are none available or given with purchases.

As we slowly looked through the assortment of items on the shelves, lo and behold, there it was. In amongst all the oil, tires, and other automobile supplies! The most beautiful, brown and yellow, foil-wrapped package! It had the words "Must Sukher" - Estonian for, you guessed it, brown sugar.

Before I realized what I was actually saying, I had breathed a very sincere prayer of thanksgiving to God for finally finding brown sugar. Have you ever thanked God for brown sugar?

One item I have never thanked God for is my _____.

PRAYER

Father God, please forgive me for taking so much for granted. I fail to thank you for so many conveniences and blessings. Today, I especially thank you for zip lock bags, aluminum foil, Pam cooking spray, and yes, brown sugar. Amen.

Thankful

hearts arouse

God's

pleasure!

45

BEAUTY FROM A BOTTLE

"Pleasing is the fragrance of your perfumes, your name is like perfume poured out." Solomon 1:3

Before coming to serve a year in Estonia, I began to consider just how important it would be for the success of my ministry to have a way of connecting with the people here. God had given me a passion for women several years ago which led to speaking, directing and attending many seminars and workshops and conferences for women.

As I was sharing my concerns before leaving the states, one of my dearest lunch pals inquired, "Will you be able to continue to wear your makeup over there? Can you buy it? What will you do, actually go out in public without makeup on?" She and I laughed together as we effortlessly tried to picture me leaving the house each day without my usual but seemingly necessary MASKS.

One morning as we were preparing to leave, I asked God just how He intended for me to meet the Estonian women. A thought came. The minute it came, I knew it was God's thought.

That's it! Instead of changing the way I look, I'll help other women learn the benefits of a beautiful "outside." The idea exploded! Morning by morning as God and I had our most serious chat of the day, He revealed new ideas to me. A few weeks later, I had the whole picture. I would provide total beauty makeovers for the Estonian women. I quickly ordered the needed cosmetics and packed them with our other belongings.

My lunch friend asked, "Can you do beauty makeovers?" "Of course," I said, "I've been doing for myself for years. Have you ever seen me without this paint job I do every morning"? She had to admit she had not, nor did she care to. Six months into the year, I have had no "outside makeovers." No platform has emerged for helping women with their "outside" beauty, but God's sense of humor is priceless. And this time the joke is on me.

God has given me no opportunity to provide "outside" beauty makeovers, but what He has provided is numerous opportunities to provide "inner beauty makeovers." God seems to be saying, "Sharon, silly girl, you have it all wrong. The way to REAL total beauty is to start with the inside. Look for inner beauty. Strive for His perfect beauty of soul and mind and spirit. First share with others what real beauty is."

Oh, don't get me wrong. I still love my lotions, creams and makeup. But beauty from a bottle doesn't last. Real beauty comes from the inside out. Real beauty comes, not from a bottle, but from the heart.

I desire more _____ in my "inner beauty."

Prayer
Father, do you really think of me as a lovely creature? Thank you for calling me your finest. Amen.

God thinks

I am

beautiful just

because I am

His

46

MY PERFECT MIRROR

*"What causes fights and quarrels among you?
Don't they come from your desires that battle
within you?"*
James 4:1

Have you ever met someone and immediately known there existed an intense likeness of personality? KP and I were like that from our first encounter at our preparatory training for coming to Estonia. She is one of our team family. A few days later my hunches were activated by observing KP's behaviors, attitudes, and beliefs as well as some annoying quirks.

A few weeks later those annoying quirks had become down right distressing. Why did I find someone I like so much so difficult and challenging? As days have turned into weeks and weeks into months of closeness, sometimes being together several times a week, has presented a special set of behaviors to ponder.

Then, after much prayer, God finally revealed a striking psychological principle I had heard many times but never been able to totally understand until now. Often we have the most difficulty with persons and their behaviors that are similar to us and our behaviors we detest the most. With six months behind us, KP and I have become very special friends, almost soul mates. God alone is to be praised! We are so thankful He blessed us with an openness to grow and learn about ourselves and each other, depending on our Father Creator's divine omniscience to guide each and every day of our "mirrored" journey.

Last evening I spent several hours listening and sharing with KP about a difficult situation she was facing. George and I shared with her how special she is to us, how much God has planned for her and much about how God has given me the grace of age to be a builder of experiences from which she may gain wisdom. We shared numerous experiences of God's patience and teaching of His wondrous love to the both of us. We had a glorious evening!

KP has taught me much about myself. And, as I have observed her annoying behaviors, those of mine that are similar have begun to dissipate, ever so slowly. Funny, so has hers! To see myself so clearly in a mirror that so closely represents me and every single one of my flaws is such a blessed, painfully productive experience. And, in addition, the gain of a lifelong soulmate in the process is sheer joy unspeakable.

Today, I want to thank you for my one true, honest "mirror" friend, _____.

Prayer

Thank you gracious Father for the gift of "my perfect mirror." Thank you for blessing and anointing our spirits as one with yours. Thank you for teaching both KP and me to model you, our perfect teacher, to first look beyond the surface and love the soul and spirit. You have given us the greatest experience of a lifetime: <u>the opportunity through others to more clearly see ourselves</u>. Amen.

If you see

the real me,

will you still

love me?

47

THE RUSSIAN SOUL

After that whole generation had been gathered to their fathers, another generation grew up, who knew neither the Lord nor what he had done for Israel. Judges 2:10

Currently, there is quite a lot of attention placed on the Russian President, Boris Yeltzin, and his new political cabinet of power brothers. With the worldwide coverage of CNN News Channel, most of us know most of what is happening in Russia and most of us wish we knew less.

Not quite so commonly known or discussed is the personal spirit of the Russian people. Often we perceive the soul of a people to be represented by the government. Not so with the Russian Soul. Since arriving in Estonia where around forty percent of the population is Russian, much of my curiosity centers around the vast diversity in the Estonian and Russian people.

During the past few days, while utilizing our cultural exchange ministry days, the dynamics of the Russian Soul has become overwhelmingly apparent through some very typical, but very special Russians. I would like to share a few profiles with you.

Appropriately, the best part of this story begins with my next door neighbor's teenage son, Maxx. Maxx accepted our invitation to accompany us to St. Petersburg. We intended this gift to be a token of our gratitude for his personal assistance in interpreting and helping us with errands that only one who speaks Russian could accomplish at our Russian post office, laundry, shopping center, and grocery store.

If the rest of what happened during our recent trip to show our son Blaine the cultural former capitol of Russia was communicated to us, it was definitely lost in the language barrier.

Inna, a high school girl friend of Maxx's mother was awaiting us at the 7 A.M. train arrival. She proceeded to coach Maxx, who in turn informed us what was transpiring. The first task was to get a taxi to get to the bus station to purchase tickets to leave for South Estonia three days later.

After that routine accomplishment, Inna became our personal tour guide, showing us every inch of the majestic St. Petersburg, ON FOOT!! And, with Inna in high heels! What really blows my mind is the strength of these Russian women. I was in tennis shoes and could not stay up with her by any stretch of the imagination. A typical female, I couldn't help noticing at the day's end, there weren't even any scratches or marks on her spotlessly clean heels. Beats me!!

Inna gave us every ounce of her mind, strength, and heart for the entire day. When we treated her to lunch, she made sure she repaid us by purchasing all our tickets for the next event. Inna invited us to spend the next night with her and her fifteen-year-old son to save hotel costs. We gratefully and politely refused. She waved good-bye and walked off as energetically as she had started. It truly amazed us all that any one human being could have exhibited so much energy on such little fuel. (To top it all off, she had taken a day away from her job to be our guide. I am still asking myself whether I would do that for a friend, and definitely whether for a stranger.)

The next day was much the same, but with a different Russian soul. Nicholas met us at the famous Hermitage Square the next morning. Nicholas was a friend of Maxx's grandmother's niece. I think they are neighbors. And typically the Russian *neighbor* is the same as family.

We were overwhelmed at the depth of interest Nicholas took in explaining the significance of all the important landmarks. He drove us up and down every street of the four and one-half million populated city. We know because our rumps ached for days from bouncing up and down over tracks, bridges, and potholes. I was certain we bounced over a few cars, dogs, and people. Nicholas was the typical European driver!

Nicholas at one point heard us talking about loving pizza, and at 6 P.M. he wheeled in front of the Pizza Hut franchise. I could have kissed his feet. Never in all my mouthwatering days have I ever wanted more to "chow down" on an American Pizza. We swapped addresses, shared cross cultural stories and jokes as we demolished much too much pizza, the best I ever had.

Nicholas decided there was enough daylight to continue our city tour. Each time as we completed viewing a landmark, we would assure him we had taken enough of his time and we could use the rest. Obviously, something was lost in the translation because a few minutes later we would pull up in front of another landmark. Finally, when the darkness overtook us, we were escorted to our hotel.

Exchanges of small talk were made by all, and we tiredly turned toward the hotel. Nicholas shouted out with a kind, but firm voice, "Hey, tomorrow is Sunday. There will be few taxis available at 5:30 A.M. I will be here to take you all to the bus station." Overwhelmed, I asked Nicholas why would one be so kind to a perfect stranger. His reply startled me. He said, "We are friends of Maxx's grandmother's aunt's family. This is our pleasure."

And sure enough, just as we had guessed, the prompt Nicholas came barreling up to a screeching halt at the agreed-upon time. Soon and very soon, we were at the bus station and bade farewells to another strangely unique, but amazingly similar beauty of Russian Soul. **A soul of much warmth, generosity, and true selflessness.** A soul I much admire.

No sooner had Nicholas departed, than Inna reappeared just to make sure we had made it okay and to wish us well on our way. I asked her if she had to work on Sunday. "No." She said she just wanted to see us off. She was fully dressed and beautiful in her - you guessed it – three-inch heels.

And now I return to Maxx. You may remember my mentioning his name at the beginning of my story. We thought we were doing him a favor by giving him the privilege of traveling with us. As it turns out, the last laugh is Maxx's, his mother's and his grandmother's.

Maxx, his grandmother and Natasha, Maxx's mother, planned the whole trip, contacting Nicholas and Inna. Maxx's agreed upon role was very obvious from the start. He was there to make the trip to the culturally profound city a stress-free, totally enjoyable trip for our family. He took complete control of all the logistics, learning the Herculean metro, buying our food, exchanging money and sacrificing landmarks he preferred.

My curious mind was completely taken aback. Why Maxx? Why would he do all this for us - almost strangers. His answer startled me as much as Nicholas' answer had. "Oh, it is nothing. Anyone would do this for you. Any Russian would do this," he said again. "Oh," I said, "because they want to represent their country proudly?" "No!" he said seriously. "Just because that's the way we Russians are."

Maxx relaxed and began to be comfortable enough to join in our joking and playing with each other. Once he stated, "Sharon, I am going to my room. I think I should warn you, when I return my humor will have awakened!" Blaine, George and I laughed and laughed with him as we assured him his humor was already awake.

Two days later we entered our flat to allow Blaine time to pack for the flight home. Maxx's grandmother, the epitome of all Russian Souls, met us at the door. She had prepared a traditional and delicious meal of wieners and Irish potatoes. She was quick to see the tiredness of every single cell in my body and insisted I lie down. She proceeded to position me a pillow and covered me with her favorite blanket. She patted and caressed me as she reminded me she was my self-designated Russian mother. I smiled and felt all the warmth she intended. Hers is a heart of love of which, over and over again we have been recipients. Hers is a typical Russian **soul of great passion and one of deep generosity** (even when it means great sacrifices of self needs). The spirit of the Russian soul is one of **verbal honor**. A **good firm handshake** or a verbal agreement is all that is ever needed. Why would one need anything further? If they say "I'll be there at 10 A.M.," they are there at 10 A.M. No excuses are allowed. Their **honesty** astounds me. Their **integrity is impeccable with directness and preciseness. They feel deep and continue reaching for that depth long after one would think sufficient.**

Truly the Russian leaders are sitting center stage in international politics. The countrymen know they are at the most critical crossroads of their volatile and rich history. The Russian people can do little that impacts everyday lives. No matter what happens to the future of their special form of democracy, the Russian spirit will not be crushed. Theirs is one of indescribable

<u>buoyancy</u>, indomitable <u>spirit</u>, impassioned <u>love</u> and <u>loyalty</u>, and indelibly lost without Christ. All the Russian soul is lacking to be a perfectly packaged partner for us who love the Lord is.... well.... our everything.... Jesus Christ our Lord.

The spirit of my soul lacks _____.

Prayer
Oh, Lord God, you have made the heavens and all the earth and her inhabitants. Would you have mercy on the Russian souls and give them a while longer? Amen.

A changed future requires a changed mind!

CONCLUSION

A few weeks after writing the devotion "Russian Soul," my ill health took its toll. After much professional consultation, prayer, and deliberation, my husband and I agreed to come home immediately to seek necessary medical attention.

Of course the year of ministry and service did not end as we had planned or even dreamed it would. We shared premature goodbyes at many teas given to honor our abrupt departure.

With a broken and sad heart, and feeling somewhat confused but with a peaceful state of mind, we boarded the plane. Almost all our new found Russian and Estonian friends, who now seemed like family, stood waving to us and shouting in their native tongues, "I will love you my forever friends."

But God in His Sovereignty always knows best. On October 1, 1997, we stepped back on American soil to almost two hundred friends and family cheering us with heartfelt hugs and kisses.

Until July of 1997, I spent most of my days in bed due to a "complete broken down immune system." Some research specialists labeled my severe illness as Systemic Lupus. Other doctors still seem baffled!

On July 13, 1997, the fervent and effectual prayer of a few godly women ushered in what was later medically documented as a "complete and total divine healing." Hallelujah!

Through it all I have learned much more about God's grace and goodness which I'll be sharing with you in intimate detail in my next book *Entering His Rest*!

May God's love be with you until we sit down together again. Enjoy your life and engage it with Him as you continue to feast on His awesome and total love. And may I suggest that you do it with a tasty cup of tea. It comes in all flavors.

Contact the author for the following:

- Schedule a speaking or teaching event
- Order books for your retreats, conferences, etc.
- Receive the Free Indeed! Newsletter
- Receive dates of future conferences
- Receive information on books in progress

Write to	Free Indeed! Ministries
	Sharon Bretherick
	2348 Mill Ridge Drive
	Montgomery, Alabama 36117
Phone	(334) 395-5848
Email	Bretherick@aol.com